SUPER NATURAL SELLING

SUPER NATURAL
SELLING
(For Everyday People)

Danielle Kennedy

Craig Publications
Danielle Kennedy Productions, Inc.
P.O. Box 4382
San Clemente, California 92672
(714) 498-8033

ISBN 0–9613396–0–8

Library of Congress Card Number: TXU 151-901

Composition and Production by Publisher's Typography

DEDICATION

On or about June 7, 1972 at approximately 10:30 P.M. I wrote the paperwork for my first sale. I was very confused, afraid and awkward with my customer. Luckily, I had a friend in sales. I slipped into a separate room and called him up whispering, "Help! What do I do? What do I say?" I didn't know it at the time but he gave me the best advice I have ever received as a salesperson: "Just be the natural you. . . ."

This book is dedicated to that friend. He was the first super natural salesperson I had ever met. Now he is my super natural husband, among other things.

To Michael Craig: "Thanks for talking to me then but mostly, thanks for loving me now."

ACKNOWLEDGMENTS

A big "thanks a million" to the following people who fill such a bright spot in my life: Claudette Albert, my right arm, who spent hours at my side editing this manuscript. Her style and sense of commitment make her light years ahead of her age. To my friends, my inspirations, who make *Super Natural Selling* come alive: Flavia Weedn—with her magical stroke; Kassie, Patti and Roberta—with their distinctive styles of dance and direction; Mary Rubenstein, Teri Duckworth, Bill Wall, Larry West and Marilyn Maxick—for their flair with color, line and shape; Merry Brady—with her down-to-earth ability to create and communicate; Andreino—for his class and culinary skills; Shirley Pepys and Sylvia Noble—for their courage to make it happen in spite of personal pain; Andy—wherever you are, for making every sale a performance; Ruth Mayer—for capturing life on the easel; Tom Hopkins—for his ability to maintain a high degree of excellence at all costs, which tends to illuminate my path as well; Patrick, E.J. and Meg McVay—for teachings learned and directions provided; Joe Barrett—whose spirit of salesmanship and survival penetrates through my spirit daily; Rose Barrett—who taught me so much but mostly how to combine talent with humility; the Kennedy and Craig kids—my constant source of motivation and material for manuscript; Michael—my friend, my mate, my partner in growth.

CONTENTS

CHAPTER 4

THE HOMEGROWN BRAND OF INTERVIEW

CHAPTER 5

THE NATURAL GLOW OF A GOOD PRESENTATION

CHAPTER 6

A NATURAL REACTION: "I OBJECT, MAYBE?"

PREFACE

I've been selling all my life and I didn't even know it. When Sister M. Basil, R.S.M. announced the "New World Catholic Newspaper Subscription Drive" was about to start in my 8th year of life, I knew I had to try to bring in the most subscriptions. Later on, cookies got me excited. Then in high school, candy bars sent me up and down the block. By the time I was in college, I was selling furniture and clothes at part-time jobs. But if anyone had said to me, "Hey, Danny, you are a salesperson," I would have said they were dead wrong. "Selling" was not my style. You have to be pushy to do that.

Don't let anyone try to talk you out of the following idea: No matter what you do in life you have to know how to sell. Most of us hate the word "SELL." Why? Do you understand what it really means? To sell an idea, product, service, song or anything requires love and commitment. That is the purpose of this book—to provide you with understanding for that type of commitment.

If you are browsing through this book now at a bookstore or at one of my seminars, please stop and buy it. But there is one requirement—you must love what you do. If you really hate your job, we don't want you selling us on anything connected with it.

You could be a doctor, lawyer, salesperson, butcher, baker, writer, actor/actress, speaker, T.V. personality, priest, nun, minister, etc. No one is excluded. If you fall into the category of a lover of your craft, you probably are already selling and don't even know it. Your "natural" enthusiasm is catching on. So all my book will do is enhance your style, speech and strategies.

I am first and foremost a salesperson. I'm proud to make that claim now that I know what it means. Only the ignorant are ashamed to admit pride in their profession. I understand that if I cannot sell what I create every day, I must not believe in what I produce. You, too, are producing things to be proud of. They are:

services, sounds, dance movements, special effects, ideas and concepts to the public and private world you live in.

If you are good, the word will get out—"What a natural." If you are great, they will call you a super natural. Enjoy reading this book and find out how easy it can be to take that stretch to super natural greatness.

Danielle Kennedy

P.S. I hope every Girl Scout and Boy Scout in the country reads this book before they hit the streets.

CHAPTER 1

THE APPROACH: OUTSTANDING OR OBNOXIOUS

The Natural Dances to the Beat of the Customer ◆ *The Natural Delivers the Song with Feeling* ◆ *If It Feels Good, the Natural Just Goes with It* ◆ *Introducing: The Super Naturals* ◆ *Cheap Imitations of the Real Thing* ◆ *Take Nothing and Turn It into Something* ◆ *Start by Strutting Your Stuff* ◆ *The Natural Is a Private Detective* ◆ *Everybody Sells Somebody Sometime*

Think of the last person who sold you a car. Do you remember that human being with fond memories? A few months ago, my husband and I went out to buy a new economy car. With all the sales training going on, I could be sure of two things: (1) Car salespeople are professional people. (2) Car salespeople will welcome the business.

Here is how the episode started out. We knew the kind of car we wanted: low mileage, low price and a basic car (with no frills). Our teenagers would be driving the car too. I called several dealerships, asking about the specific car we wanted and the list price. This one fellow particularly excited me. He said, "Well, this car usually goes for $5,300, but if *you come in today*, I can get it for you for a lot less." Being half Irish and half cheap, I jumped on his offer.

Scene two: My husband and I were standing in the lot with the chap who said he was going to "sell it to us for less." He showed us the car and we took it for a test drive. My son Joe was egging us on. "Great, Mom, I love it. Wow, did you hear what he said?

1

50 miles to the gallon." At this point, 18-year-old Joe would have raved about a camel, if he knew that was his last way to get around town. We finally said to the salesman, "Well, you mentioned over the phone we could get it for less than $5,300. How much less?" The salesperson replied in an aggravated tone (after all, he had spent about 15 minutes of his time with us and we hadn't given him $5,000 yet), "Well, are you going to buy the car today?" We said, "Well that depends on what the price is and the figures you give us." He asked again, "Are you going to buy this car today or not?" I was getting upset. Standing in the foreground were two or three other rude individuals like him, just staring at us. I felt the vibes, "Let's see if these losers pop the big bucks or not." Finally, my husband asked, "Can we sit down and see how this works out?" The salesperson took us into his closing booth and worked out a sheet full of numbers at the $5,300 price. "These are the figures without tax and licensing and no radio, etc." We then asked, "How much off of that can we get it for, as you suggested on the phone?" He then pulled amnesia on us. His reply was, "I don't know. I'll have to ask my boss."

Scene three: The salesman left the room. My husband said, "When he was asking us if we could buy the car today, I should have asked him if he could sell us the car today." For your own information, not too many car salespeople can sell a car. They usually have to check it out with their manager. If they can't do it on their own, a T.O. (take-over) person comes in and works you over. This human being can be pushy and intimidating or polite and accommodating. The salesman came back and asked, "How are you going to pay for this car?" My husband replied, "If the price is good, we might pay cash." The salesman left again. When he returned, he acted put out and said, "There is just no way we can sell you this car for under $5,500." First he lured us in and then he joked us around for one hour, and then he came back with this message. And who was he getting the message from? God? I pictured this big strong-armed person sitting in a smoke-filled room yelling, "Nail those idiots you fool, nail 'em."

This is a pretty discouraging sight. We had the money and the intention to buy a car that day. We were so mad and upset that we just left and went home. Finally, we purchased a car from what I would call a "natural." That is what this book is all about—naturals and how they sell. The approach a salesperson has on the phone or in person starts the ball rolling. It is no different than a singles bar scene. If you go to a bar, you usually do not have to talk to the most obnoxious individual in the place. Often times, when you buy a product, you *think* you have no choice.

Looking back, it is hard to believe that I consider myself a salesperson and am proud of it. Based on my childhood and young adult experiences, selling was hardly the field I intended to pursue. Salespeople had cigars, loud booming voices and only one thing on their mind—taking your money. I got my first taste of salespeople at the door of my mom's house. When I was about eight years old, Mom had to have an operation in the hospital. When she returned home to recuperate, she would nap in the afternoon. I can remember one day someone pounding on the door at around 2:00 p.m. I thought Mother was asleep. Then I heard her whisper to me from the other room: "Don't open the door, Danielle! It's probably that salesman." I had no idea what she meant by "that salesman," but I didn't question Mom. I figured a salesman must not be on the side of the angels.

Several years later, I had a similar experience as a new mother. New mothers don't get a whole lot of sleep in the middle of the night. I really looked forward to the nap time in the afternoon. I remember this one day in particular. I was sleeping like a baby, when suddenly I heard a doorbell. Half asleep, I got the impression that someone was pressing the bell over and over. I jumped with fright. Caught off guard, I opened the door. There was a salesman standing there yelping, "Well, how are you doing today? Do you know how many times in America women suck up absolutely no dirt into their vacuum cleaners on a day-to-day basis?" I was stunned. I still couldn't respond very well so he hit me again harder. This time he said, "Excuse me," and walked past me into the living room with a suitcase in hand.

"Now I don't know what kind of vacuum cleaner you use. I can just tell it ain't doing the job." I didn't want him to know that I wasn't even pushing the vacuum so I shut up. He then proceeded to drop a half a bag of dirt on my carpet. About then, the baby started to cry from the nursery. I was beginning to get this whole picture. I was tired and confused and wanted this nut out of my house. I excused myself to get the baby. When I returned, he was pulling out this elaborate vacuum system and started to plug it in and show me how great this machine can suck up dirt. By then, I had a headache.

Some of you are probably saying: "Come on sweetie, couldn't you have stopped him at the door?" I was not good at saying no at that stage of the game and I was half asleep. He was only interested in one thing—selling his product. He had no awareness of the customers or their state of mind, etc. I finally got him out of there by saying I had to feed my baby and couldn't afford a vacuum. He, of course, was going to come back when the "man of the house" was home on Saturday!

Here I was, resisting salespeople, not realizing that I was doing my own brand of selling since I sold my first subscription to a newspaper at the age of nine. Was I rude and insensitive just like the salesperson at my mom's door a long time ago? In high school I ran for office and won votes. Was I selling myself? I made a lot of phone calls and shook a lot of hands. How about the furniture I sold in the summer of my senior year in high school? During the month of July I received the top sales award. Later in college I found myself once again selling. This time the products were clothes. Through all of this I never referred to myself as a sales-person. That was beneath me. After all I was going to college and maybe someday become an actress, writer or some type of profes-sional. I thought most salespeople didn't have an education, were the "pushy" type and made people feel generally uncomfortable. I didn't do things like that. In grade school, I wasn't selling. I was trying to win a contest. In high school, I wasn't selling. I was making friends and gaining votes. At the furniture store, I wasn't selling. I was counseling people who were interested in purchasing a sofa. In college, God knows, I wasn't selling. I was coordinating wardrobes.

Who was I trying to kid? Where did I get the idea selling was so bad? Maybe that one afternoon at the age of 7 or 21. But I was dead wrong. If I felt that way, how many more people, especially young people, get this stereotyped image of salespeople in their heads? How many natural salespeople have we lost to the structured job position because "I could never do the things that salespeople do." Then later in life, because colleges do not adequately educate students about the world of selling, people realize they hate their jobs but refuse to make a career change because they fear they are too old. Inside of that person is a frustrated sales star dying to be born but afraid to risk the "label" that the profession connotes.

I have a very dear friend who had her doctorate in science and spent thirty years in a laboratory. She told me for almost 20 of those 30 years she dreamed of getting into selling. But her mother would have killed her if she did. After all, she had gone to great expense educating her for this prestigious career and if she dropped out of this profession it would be a disappointment to the family. She finally did drop out and become a super, natural sales star. For 10 years she never told her aging mother that she had quit her research job. Finally before her mother died, my friend had become quite wealthy and gave her mother an expensive gift. "How can you afford this?" Mom asked. She then told her that she had quit her other job 10 years ago and gone into selling. Mom's reply was, "If that is what you love, then do it with my blessings." How often she has asked herself, "Why did I wait?"

At the age of 27, I needed a job. But I knew that I would hate working from 9 to 5 and be told I could only have a raise once a year. At home, I was the mother of four children under 7 years of age (two of which were in diapers) and guess what? I was pregnant with my fifth baby. I wondered who would hire me six months along in a pregnancy? Then I stopped and realized that if I got into sales nobody would have to hire me but me! So I started interviewing myself. Was I a self-starter? Did I like risk and growth opportunities? Could I juggle my prospect calls between family time? Was this a chance to have it all? Yes. I was young and I am so glad I chose sales. So many wait because of some crazy notion they have about this profession. Selling has, for me, made everything possible, both financially and emotionally. I hope young people read this. Salespeople *are* educated—some of the best. Plus, there is no reason to wait. You, like my friend, may be sorry you did.

THE NATURAL DANCES TO
THE BEAT OF THE CUSTOMER

So how did I handle this strange new world of sales? Was I obnoxious? What did I do to get the toe in the door? First off, let me say I didn't know what to *say.* I had no training and I felt like I was walking down a dark tunnel and there was no light at the end. People said door knocking was the way to go but nobody ever really said if it would pay off. I had to try. I began asking questions of myself: Do you like talking to strangers on the phone who treat you like their best friend but aren't even an acquaintance? Do you like being awakened from a nap with a jolt? Do you like to talk to pushy people during the dinner hour? Then I became my own devil's advocate. I asked myself: Do you ever like people delivering their services to you at home? Do you like the convenience of selecting something in your own territory as opposed to jumping in a car and going there. I sure do. I hate the inconvenience of shopping. I hate traffic.

I love having travel agents deliver tickets to me. Often, someone will appear at my door when I run out of cleaning products or skin moisturizer. That saves me time. People often come to our office to demonstrate their wares. This can eliminate a plane flight for us sometime. There are a million things salespeople do but one of the things that turns me on is convenience. They make things more convenient. Aha! That's the word I was searching for—*convenience.* Salespeople make life easier. They provide service in our sometimes congested day. They dance to our music. They put on our tap shoes and do the foot work. Hey! I can live with this concept. I can see that salespeople aren't all big pains in the you know where. As a matter of fact, a whole bunch of them ought to be canonized saints for the way they go out of their way for us.

THE NATURAL DELIVERS THE SONG WITH FEELING

Next I thought about the fact that it's not so much what you sing but how you sing it. Have you ever noticed vocalists really take a song and deliver it right from their heart to your insides? How many singers have mouthed the song "You Don't Bring Me Flowers Anymore?" And then there is Streisand. Get your hanky out. She's going for the throat. You're sold on the singer and the song. She also makes you feel like she has been there. Streisand has hit the bottom with you. She is in your shoes.

Now, let's apply this idea to sales. Picture this. A woman (it was me) appears at your door at about lunch time (that's a safe hour) or before 5:OO P.M. so as not to interrupt meal plans. She is six months pregnant and she has a "giveaway" in her hand. It is a rain hat. It may be raining out. If it is, she says, "I hope I am not interrupting anything (with a question in her voice). I could come back at a better time, if you prefer." Pause. "Well I am here to give you this rain hat in case you are getting your hair done today and want to stay dry but also to say that if you ever need the services I provide, I hope you will remember me. I am a full-time, commited representative, I live in this community, and I know my product very well." No matter what the product, the script works. Try "If you ever need the services of a good cosmetic lady, vacuum man, computer representative or insurance agent, remember me." That was the first high note I hit in selling. I wasn't Streisand yet, but it shattered a little glass! Maybe because I was pregnant. Maybe people felt sorry for me. Or maybe because I was just out there being me. It sure worked.

IF IT FEELS GOOD, THE NATURAL WON'T FIGHT IT

Most people thought going out in the rain was dumb, but for me it paid off. Everyone was home in the rain and they must have thought, "Look at this poor pregnant thing; she is really dedicated." They would always ask me in and the next thing you know, we would begin striking up a friendship and I would find out the most amazing things. More about that in chapter 3. I found the "natural" way for me to feel comfortable about prospecting and it worked.

As time went on, I discovered the vacuum cleaner salesperson who shoved was usually short lived in the profession of selling. The greats were masters at finesse. I started watching people in my field who excelled and they were the most caring, loving people I had ever met. I have to say, they are definitely different breeds of cat. They are creative and will take risks that most won't. They seem awfully happy and free because they follow their intuition and it usually works and all of them seem to have their own style.

INTRODUCING: THE SUPER NATURALS

Take Sylvia Noble who started sewing baby blankets out of her garage with her vivacious partner Shirley Pepys in the late 60's. Sylvia is a fiery, passionate and loving Italian. Shirley is a warm, soft-spoken lady's lady. Together, they sold Bullocks (a major Southern California department store) on putting a few of their infant seat covers in the baby department to see if they would sell. Twelve years later their infant seat covers, baby blankets and baby wall hangings are everywhere. Their NoJo Corporation is a 10-million-dollar business. I asked these women how they sold the first couple of infant seat covers. You got it: the natural way. "We don't know what your customers will think of these but our friends love them. Would you put a few out and see what your customers think? What do you think? Do we have a chance?" Knowing those two, it wouldn't have mattered whether one strange person thought the product had a chance or not. They were going to make sure someone, somewhere, heard their news. They loved their product and that's all that mattered.

Next is Flavia Weedn. Flavia is one of the greats in the field of art. Here's a letter from her regarding the selling of her early paintings:

I began selling my paintings in open art exhibits in the early 1960's and a short time later my husband and I were doing it fulltime. Paintings were selling so quickly that soon pegboard covered our living room walls so that we'd have more hanging space for paintings to dry. I remember once even having to spread some work out on the roof to keep a deadline for a large L.A. department store order. Within a few years we were involved with galleries, contracts for reproduction on cards, calendars, licensing agreements, etc. One of the frustrations I found during this time was trying to hold on to the direction of my work. Because my work is so personal, as it illustrates an expression of my philosophy, its direction is important. When others tried to change this direction, I felt like a puppet whose strings were being pulled the wrong way. We now have our own publishing firm, Roserich Designs Ltd. Our children, who have not only grown up with my art, but who also share my philosophy, are principals in the company and are dedicated to nurturing this direction.

The greatest obstacle I had to overcome was to rid myself of overwhelming feelings of inferiority concerning my work in the beginning. Because I was mostly self-taught, I was always self-conscious when I showed my work and continued to be surprised that there was such a demand for it. My background had been only the basic fundamentals of art and this tremendous love and desire to express myself—but I had no formal training. I remember well my initial feelings at that first art show when I saw all the professionals around me. I kept taking the paintings in and out of the trunk of my car before I finally set up. At the end of the day, one artist whose work I admired, said to me, "Flavia, I hope you keep painting—your work has a kind of magic because it sings. And that's the ingredient most artists strive for." During the 20 years since that statement, I have met and worked with many schooled technicians who are very well skilled and yet whose work has no magic. It's been lost somewhere or overshadowed by what they've been taught. So, for me, being self-taught was a tremendous advantage. I developed my own style and because I was unafraid to let myself be vulnerable, my work had imagination and feeling. I thank God I had courage enough to take a risk in the beginning, and am reminded of what might have happened if I hadn't taken my paintings out of my car that day, by a quote from Oliver Wendell Holmes:

> *"Alas for those who never sing, but die*
> *with all their music still in them."*

Flavia had no training. Sometimes we use the lack of training as an excuse not to go out there and dig. But often the intuition and the magic of our style can be overshadowed by rote ways to do things. Flavia didn't realize it at the time but she couldn't just create. She, her husband, Jack, or someone had to promote. Most artists understand that creation and promotion must go hand in hand. That makes the whole concept even scarier. Because not only must we believe in our own creation, but we must also have the confidence that others will too.

One of the really important messages about my training is: Keep your natural, intuitive style. And add some of the tips I give you to produce even greater results. The second part of my training usually means giving you a kick in the pants. It took Flavia's husband, Jack, to convince her she should go sell her stuff. It took Sylvia and Shirley together, convincing each other to keep plugging. The naturals need a push because they are humble. As my husband so often says to me, "You aren't Danny Kennedy on that stage; you are Peter Pan, flying the gang off to the world of 'Yes I can, I can, I can.' And they leave knowing you can and so can they." What else could we possibly do for each other?

CHEAP IMITATIONS OF THE REAL THING

We talked about a couple of naturals. It might be wise to mention examples of the not so natural types. Why? Because it builds our awareness and helps cut out some of the things that we do to ourselves to become our own and the public's worst enemy. I can remember one day visiting a stereo store needing some mini cassette tapes for my recorder. It was three o'clock on a Friday afternoon. The normal business hours of this stereo store were 9:00 A.M. to 5:00 P.M. I never thought they might be closed. When I arrived at the door, a white sign was taped to the outside. "Please come back in fifteen minutes." I looked in the window. There was a salesperson behind the counter poring madly over paperwork and answering the phone a mile a minute. I was in a hurry and needed the tapes to take on a trip. I tapped on the window. He kept waving me away as he walked towards me. "Can't you see I am closed for fifteen minutes? I have too much paperwork and too many phone calls to make right now. I can't handle anymore

customers." You probably thought I was going to describe salespeople like we talked about in the beginning of the chapter, people
who try to force their product down our throats. Included among
the obnoxious are those thousands of individuals who have to be
forced to take our money. They would rather be sitting behind a
desk or left alone in a laboratory to stare at mice. THEY DON'T
LIKE WORKING WITH THE PUBLIC. And quite frankly, their
approach is worse than the individuals who are trying to push
their way into our lives.

By the way, I came back fifteen minutes later. (Boy, am I a
pushover.) This time when I told him what I wanted, he took me
to the back of the store and showed me this huge shipment of
boxes that were just delivered. He claimed the mini cassettes were
in the bottom box and he wouldn't have time to unpack. I always
tell my salespeople "Please sell to people that want to buy." But
the consumer has to beware too. The consumer needs to buy from
people who want to sell. This guy couldn't have cared less.

TAKE NOTHING AND TURN IT INTO SOMETHING

Most salespeople who are considered obnoxious by the public are
either lazy or fearful. You can tell because they do everything in
their power to discourage folks from approaching them. In my
programs, I talk about the salesperson with his feet up on the desk
eating a sandwich, praying no one comes by asking for anything.

The natural turns that nothing into a something. That's why
the complainers always think the great salespeople have extra
business being handed to them. They do. They have extra business
from all the somethings out there. The somethings that were turned
into nothings by the negative salesperson. Here is what the naturals do. They approach customers with a friendly greeting, give
them something to keep (like a sample of their product) and then
proceed to walk them to the door saying the following words: "If
you ever need additional information regarding my product or
services, feel free to call at anytime. Please remember me." Let's
examine the circumstances here for a moment. The customers
ended up in our office or store because they were lost and wanted

to find their way to a party. Most negative salespeople see these type of customers as intruders. This can even happen at a gas station. The gas attendant represents his boss's station and can do a lot of great customer relations for that boss with the right attitude.

Maybe the individuals that were lost now arrive at the party. Someone at that party wonders why they were late. Bango. That starts the conversation in your direction. These total strangers are spreading good rumors about you. They say, "Well you see, we were lost and we ended up at this stereo store (or gas station, real estate office or bank). This great salesperson or attendant handed us a map, a free sample of their product, a brochure, and some friendly advice on how to get to your party." By coincidence there is someone at that party that needs something from that service. By these strangers bringing up the location or store, it reminded them that they needed to buy something. They end up giving this person your name, card, phone number or whatever. The next thing you know you end up with a new customer. You took a nothing and changed it to something. What a special effect artist. Meanwhile back at the ranch, the sluggish salesman is half asleep and praying no one interrupts his nap. The first thing I am trying to rid you of are false assumptions. We received those false assumptions because of bad experiences with salespeople we encountered. Let's assume that we each ran up against the something/nothing type of salesperson. Let's take it a step further and say this type of individual is basically unhappy in his or her profession. That means they can't strut their stuff. How can you sell and show off, if you are not proud of what you do? Or how can you sell, if no one has taught you what to do? Wouldn't you sit in fear all day? I would. So let's break down the problem and work on strutting your stuff first.

START BY STRUTTING YOUR STUFF

Recently, an actress came to Hollywood and visited a major talent agency. She figured, because she was loaded with talent, her venture into show business would be a snap. One of the questions the agent asked her was "How do you feel about door to door selling?" She hated it and felt it was beneath her. The talent agent told her to go back home and get a regular job. Because it doesn't matter how much talent you have. She was not willing to go out on one audition, one interview or one lead after another. The people who have survived in the entertainment field have had to have the same determination any salesperson has about his or her product and you *can't* give up if you believe in your product.

Let's face it, I don't care what your profession is, you are selling something. It might be your ideas at a board meeting, a hamburger presented in McDonald's or a smile at the receptionist desk. Every major effort in our economy started with a basic super natural sale being made to someone. Our history is built on selling skills. If we can't conquer the fear of approach with the public in some shape or form, we might as well hole up in our closets for the rest of our lives. Flavia said it beautifully. She almost didn't open up her trunk.

And do you know what is amazing? People often think the typical salesperson is an egotistical maniac. Egotistical usually means someone who centers everything around him or herself. How can the super natural salesperson be egotistical? At some point in this book, you will begin to understand that these individuals are busy giving and contributing to the public. It calls for high concentration and tremendous sensitivity of what the customer needs. People who are frightened, worried and insecure are egotistical. They think they are so important that most of their day should be fretting over their pimples. Who has time to expand and stretch and look into the eye of another human being who may need our help?

Just for clarification let's compare the obnoxious to the outstanding in the field of super natural selling:

Obnoxious	**Outstanding**
Tries to use force	Tries to determine needs
The goal: The commission	The goal: The customer's future business
Usually resents people	Usually is a "people person"
Says *I* a lot	Says *you* a lot

Obnoxious (*continued*)	**Outstanding** (*continued*)
Backs people into corners and secretly laughs	Backs people out of uncomfortable places.
"Has to" make the sale (operates under scarcity)	Doesn't "have to" have anything (there is plenty of business to go around)
Walks in cold turkey	Understands the importance of pre-approach information
Gets impatient when people don't buy today.	Works patiently with the customer
Won't share with other salespeople and is jealous.	Knows that he or she is the only true competition.

THE NATURAL IS A PRIVATE DETECTIVE

The natural sale falls into place because of the ability of the pro to *research* and *investigate* the prospect whenever possible prior to the initial approach. We call this *pre-approach* behavior. Even when applicants are selling themselves at job interviews, they understand that prior to the appointment, it's a good idea to learn about the company, product and general style of the group. We'll talk more about job interviewing and selling yourself in chapter four. Likewise, the salesperson who is about to sell his or her product to the customer will do the same thing.

If I want to sell a computer to a company, I will definitely bone up before the contact meeting. So it beehoves me, as the professional salesperson, to gather information regarding what this company does and how my product can facilitate things for them. Then during the course of our discussion, I can insert certain *scripts* and bits of information about their company, which I have discovered. For instance: "I understand that the costs of mailing lists and storage of files have added thousands of dollars to your company's yearly expenses. With this computer we can store hundreds and hundreds of names and addresses along with pertinent information regarding these customers on small disks. At a moment's notice, we can pop one in and get the answer we need, without searching three blocks over in a storeroom or warehouse for the information."

I derived the specific information about their company during an informational interview two days before. It went something like this: I called the company and explained to the switchboard operator that I was scheduled to come in soon for a presentation on computers and who the presentation was with. I then asked her for the secretary's name of the gentleman I was going to see. I asked her to buzz me into the secretary. At this point, I tried this approach: "Hi, Mary. We don't know each other yet, but I am due in for an appointment with Mr. Smith this week. I am preparing some things regarding the presentation and your company now. I know how busy Mr. Smith is and I hate to waste anyone's time. Knowing you are right in the middle of all the action, can you please tell me what specifically your company would most need a computer for? Where are you losing time right now in your operation? Where does a computer fit in? Your input would be most valuable!"

Two things work here: (1) I now have the secretary feeling wanted. Building rapport with her is critical, if I am to build rapport with her boss. (2) I am getting smart real fast on the company's product and the needs of that company. I may want to ask her some questions about what this company is doing right. I understand that "flattery will get me everywhere" at the initial interview. There is nothing worse than a hot shot salesperson coming into a company and trying to tell old standbys (people who have done something the same way for years) how wrong they are. Let's face it, they have done a lot right or they wouldn't be there today. My job is to show them how my product can make the load a little lighter and more effective. Pre-approach information is a must for the direct, on line salesperson. If we get a referral about someone who needs our product, it is important that we ask the referral specifically what needs the lead has: "Thanks so much, Mary, for telling me about Gwen, who may need some makeup. Does she have any allergies? What price has she been paying for her makeup and is a budget in the picture?" Mary may know some of the answers or none at all. But you must ask.

If you are going out for the first time to meet the customer and you don't have a whole lot of information, please be observant. Perhaps you are going door to door. You walk up the path and notice a beautifully manicured lawn. Maybe the garage door is open and you see a pair of water or snow skis leaning up on the side of the garage. At the door you can use this little observation and conversation starter. "Hi, Mrs. Quick, I see you all like to water ski." She says, "Oh, you noticed our skis. Yes, as a matter of fact, we just returned from a fun water ski trip in Lake Shasta." "No kidding," you reply, "my family went up there last year." She immediately doesn't see you as someone selling something, but a person with a family. I think it is important, at the approach, to begin a *natural conversation*. Throwing them with some pre-approach information always seemed to get the ball rolling in a much more comfortable fashion. By the time you tell her you are with Beauty, Inc., you are a person first and saleswoman second.

This also applies to the salesperson calling on corporate clients. Look at your surroundings. Are you waiting in the vice president's office? Do you see family photos? Sports certificates? Memorabilia? Be alert, aware, curious and interested. Believe me, if you are in the present moment, it's natural to see what's in front of you. When you have plenty of time to research prior to the initial contact, please do it. As a sales trainer, I do my research in the following manner. When I am asked to speak to a group of people who sell a particular product, I want to give them information that will definitely increase their productivity. I may never have sold that product personally, but if I do not use any real life circumstances that pinpoint how these methods can help them, they don't relate as fast. Long before a presentation, we will have the secretary to president send us their training manual, product brochures and anything else that can aid me. For instance, last year I spoke to a group of people who sell china, crystal and cookware on the party plan. My first question was "What market specifically do you appeal to?" I found out it was single working women. These women could well afford nice table settings and cookware, so why wait until marriage? They may as well start now and enjoy. So, I proceeded to learn each and every product backwards and forwards and then created a group of scripts that their salespeople could use both before, during and after the initial and follow-up appointments. The biggest compliment I had was at the end of the day. The president of the company came up to me and said: "Not only did you give us our money's worth, but we felt like you had been marketing our product for years. We thought we were listening to one of our top salespeople." That all came from doing homework.

As a student of the Catholic schools, all through my education the good nuns continually gave me the following advice: "Do your homework." Many of my friends who went to public school, came home at 3:00 P.M. and could go out and play. But no, not me. I had homework. Today, I am grateful because I use this skill in selling. Remember how horrible it was as a child to have a test in school (maybe a surprise quiz) and you did awful because you hadn't done your homework? Well, going out on a sales presentation with little or no information about the customer gives you that same sinking feeling, especially when the customer does most of the questioning and you realize you don't know much.

Get smart fast about your customer. Before the initial interview, have information regarding the following things:

The Company   How long has it been in existence? Who started the company? Most companies have an interesting rags to riches story about their growth. Find out who the builders and champions were. Find out if they are still around. Find out about any idiosyncracies the company may have. Maybe they have a certain dress code. Find out about charities or institutions they support. For instance, Southland Corporation and Electronicis Realty Association are big contributors to Jerry Lewis's Muscular Dystrophy campaign. You can drop a statement in the approach appointment about their involvement.

The Job of the Person You Are Talking to   What does the person you are talking to do? Be inquisitive about them and be able to drop some information about their work during the interview.

Their Hobbies   Know them. Golf particularly. People that golf all stick together. If you both golf, you may have a hot discussion going. Tennis, aerobics, racquetball, etc.

What They Intend to Use Your Product for and in What Department of the Company   Have they used something similar? Competitors? Why are they changing? Is this the first time out for using this type of product?

Mutual Friends   Is this a lead from a mutual friend? This is an excellent rapport builder during the approach and if you know that information ahead of time it helps, especially if they are fond of the mutual friend and that person has a great deal of credibility in their eyes. Often, I was able to make the sale not because of the closing skills I showed, but because of a mutual friend. Thank God, I didn't blow it at the approach meeting. The attitude of my customer was: "Well, Sam just goes on and on about you. If you can handle Sam, you can handle anyone. That's all I need to know."

Pricing, Price Ranges, Budgets   Is cost a factor? If so try to find out beforehand. All my landscape architects out there—carpenters, brick masons and decorators—listen up. It beehoves you to know what you are working with. It helps during the presentation because you don't scare them off when you come back with your bids.

Get A Handle on the Tempo of the Customer   Do you know beforehand if the people are formal or casual? I am thinking about our decorator, Merry Brady, when I write this. When she works with her customers, she definitely keys into their lifestyle and attitudes and builds her designs and plans around that. She really uses a lot of honesty regarding the practicality of a piece of furniture or a treatment when presenting it. Merry is not out to gouge people financially, even if she knows they have the bucks. I can remember when we were working on doing some things to the inside of our new house. Merry made comments like, "Danny, are you crazy? The kids will have that fabric worn out in a month.

Look at this one. It's so much more inexpensive, looks smart and will serve the purpose. Let's put the extra bucks into a sub-zero refrigerator. With this family you need it."

I have watched other decorators in action. All they had in mind was spend, spend, spend. And the practicality or lifestyle of the people was never taken into consideration. Merry will sit with us in the middle of the bedroom floor while designing a bedroom style for us and say, "You people are so relaxed and beachy. This room should be uncluttered and easy the way you two are. And the colors should also express that." She is not only our decorator but our friend. She has spent nights eating tacos and drinking beer with us at the kitchen table with children flying around. She knows the way we live and can adapt a plan to meet that. I love a salesperson who rolls their sleeves up and gets into pre-approach information before they try to appear for the real thing.

EVERYBODY SELLS SOMEBODY SOMETIME

If there is one thing I want you to start out remembering as we journey through *Super Natural Selling* it's *everybody sells somebody sometime*. You could be selling yourself on a job interview. You may be selling your product, your services or your ideas to the advertising department. Are you selling homes, lifestyles, cosmetics, cars, services or your talents to a producer? The list goes on and on. Somewhere in this book you are going to have to get acceptance from yourself that "selling ain't bad." Shoving is bad. Pushy is bad. But you say, "I like intimidation and squirming now and then." That tells me you didn't feel comfortable enough with either yourself or the product, so you push and not let it flow naturally. Learn more about yourself, your reactions and your product. This will block the shove and ease the nerves. That's what I want to help you with in the following chapters. If you are doing something you believe in, you have to sell it. In writing this book, I knew the word *selling* had to be in the title. Why? Because first and foremost, I am a salesperson. And yet the public seems to shy away from the word itself. However, the American economy's best friend is the salesperson. Usually, when people describe a good one, they say things like, "They aren't pushy. They are so unaffected. So real. I feel like I have known them half my life. They are naturals." Everything today stresses the natural. People eat natural foods. No one likes artificial additives or preservatives. We like the fresh, natural taste.

The word *super* has been used and abused. Everyone ran out of words for a while when they got excited about something and just said "Super." Then we got *Superman*. Followed by *Superman II*. Next came *Superman III*. To me, Superman was pretty special. He had extra powers and graces to help people. We weren't just talking about some ordinary guy. We were talking about a SUPER guy!! Wow! Pow! Wham!

Well guess what? You take the word *super,* then the word *natural* and put it in front of the word salesperson and you are going to get the likes of SUPERMAN and SUPERWOMAN in the sales field. But you must add natural because these people are fresh, graceful and very ordinary people leading extraordinary lives. You heard about Flavia, Sylvia Noble, Shirley Pepys and Merry Brady. Scattered throughout this book, there are more. And they come from every walk of life. Most books describe celebrity sales stars that everyone knows. I decided to talk about the super naturals in my own back yard—people that you don't know personally, but yet carry a strange resemblance to people you do business with on your side of the world. Guess why? There are super naturals everywhere. All you have to do is look around. They are so good at what they do, you don't even know you are being sold. You are. I am. And it is absolutely great. Let's see how it's done, naturally.

CHAPTER **2**

THE SUPER NATURAL PLAN

Meet the Crazy Lady with Scratch Paper ♦ *Don't Go Nuts and Get Complicated on Me* ♦ *Learn the Three New Steps to Activity: Begin, Continue and Complete* ♦ *Sister Mary Ignatius Says: Do Your Homework the Night Before* ♦ *Don't Be So Nosey When You First Wake Up* ♦ *What Day Is Today? Touch Your Nose. Pull Your Ear* ♦ *Clean Up the Past. Burn It Now* ♦ *Public Enemy #1 Is You. Interview Yourself Barbara Walters* ♦ *Starting and Completing. Are You a Beginner, a Mover or an Ender?*

W hen a gymnast is out on the exhibition floor, notice how he or she twists, turns, jumps and lands so gracefully. It looks so easy. People observing will say, "The kid's a natural." Then they drop the conversation and watch the next performer. My son Kevin is a gymnast. People do not realize the hours of preparation, development, time planning and physical and mental endurance that this sport requires. Watching him grow as a gymnast has taught me so many lessons about life. He does absolutely everything the coach tells him to do plus he loves the sport passionately. He eats right, sleeps well, practices daily at the gym, lifts weights and never misses a practice or a class. The list goes on and on. He takes the bus thirty miles by himself to get to the gym. He is very self-motivated. But Kevin still hits "plateaus." Plateaus take you down emotionally and affect your physical performance. They happen when you least expect it. Usually they hit when you are riding high and progressing beautifully at a certain level of excellence.

This autumn, Kevin cleaned up the awards at a gymnastics meet and performed exceptionally well. But by December, he noticed

21

his workouts at the gym going wrong. He didn't land a trick right. Twisted into a move with bad timing. And mentally he began to suffer. He began worrying tremendously. Am I really good enough to go public with this sport? Have I got the strength? Have I got the talent? Am I wasting my time? Will I end up injured and hurt? He kept taking himself out of the present moment during his workouts by worrying about what he had just done wrong in the immediate past or what could go wrong in the future.

One day his coach called me and said he was in a plateau and really down and would I be aware of that and talk to him. I tried to explain to Kevin what was happening to him. Kevin talked about what happens to him when he is doing floor work. Floor work is done on mats that are laid on the ground. It involves somersaults in the air, some dance movements and a lot of co-ordination. Several tricks happen real fast on the floor. You can't stop to worry about what you just did. You must go forward. Kevin felt that if his first trick went bad, then it was downhill from there. Listening to Kevin reminded me of my problems and yours. As super salespeople, we are our own worst "present time" problem each day. What's the answer? The closest thing I can think of is the time plan. My philosophy of managing time has a lot to do with self-awareness. This means living right now as opposed to what's gone on in the past or what may happen in the future. Like Kevin, we have no time to look back. As a successful salesperson, I have had to fight being "pulled off the moment" for years. Hopefully, this chapter will give you some insight into yourself and your super, natural plan. The super naturals make everything look easy but there is much behind-the-scenes action that occurs. Let's take a peek at the millions of details connected to this wonderful world of selling.

I would like you to observe the three *circles of necessity* which every salesperson must tangle with on a day to day and week to week basis. You will notice all three circles are the same size. That's done for a reason. All three areas take priority and one circle cannot function without the other. Especially notice that without your attention on the first circle the other two would be non-existent. Now notice below what happens to the new sales-

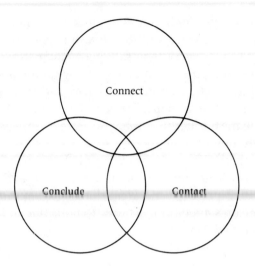

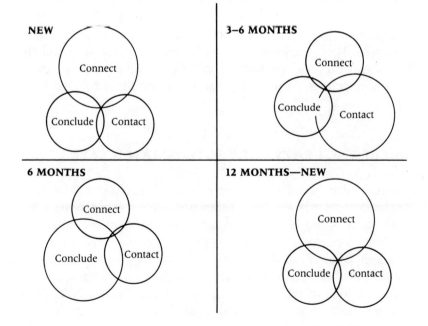

person after a six-month period of putting too much attention of time in the wrong places: (This can also happen to the pro.)

As you can see, every new salesperson starts out very enthusiastically building their credibility, talking on the phone, writing letters of introduction about themselves and their product and following up on leads. Then it happens. If you work the connection and develop the business territory you are *going to make the contacts*. This usually puts the salesperson in a tizzy. "Wow, Yipee! They like me. I struck a note. Hooray." But in the rush of excitement, time got away from them. Appointments (some good, some bad) ate up all their priority time. Next thing that happens is some of the salesperson's appointments turn to bona fide orders and they are stuck in the office servicing and concluding those orders. Following up until the customers get delivery is important. If they happen to come from a teaching background, they pay way too much attention to details. The orders have been handled, but future business is lost. That is why most salespeople always feel like they are walking on the edge. When the last order is filled, they say to themselves, "Will I ever see the whites of another customer's eyes again? I am doomed." Half of that feeling is guilt because they know they've been coasting on past business for six months. They are what I call in the intensive care unit and the only way they will get well again is to start all over. Be aware of the three circles of necessity and try to maintain balance in all three areas.

MEET THE CRAZY LADY WITH SCRATCH PAPER

When I first began my selling career, I had no idea what time management was all about. Efficiency to me meant having a 25-foot cord in my kitchen. I could swing this cord around while talking to prospects and still stir spaghetti at the stove. I also had millions of pieces of scratch paper all over the place. These things stuck out of everywhere. I had them magnetized to my refrigerator, stuck inside my car seat and attached to my blouse. I even wrote on my hand. When I perspired, I couldn't read the address that I had written on my hand.

Somebody told me about this intricate time planner that I should have. "You've got to get organized." Organized always meant structure to me. Organized always meant stick-in-the-mud to me. Time planning to me just had to be too complex. To verify my thinking, when I went out to look at time planners, everything I saw was complicated. Of course, I went out and bought this $160.00 planner just to reinforce the difficulty of this business of time planning. You should have seen this thing. It was thicker than the encyclopedia. You needed an interpreter to figure out how to use it. Guess what happened? I ended up transferring my little pieces of paper into this gold plated planner. I ask you, "Should you and I have to give up our little pieces of paper?" Finally, I decided to design my own time planner and it is full of pockets that can house little pieces of paper. And by the way, it doesn't cost $160.00. A lot of salespeople I train love it. Write me and I'll tell you how you can get one. (See pages 28–32.)

DON'T GO NUTS AND GET COMPLICATED ON ME

So, here is the point, gang. Let's keep this time planning thing simple. Everything I give you in this chapter should be *usable.* I do not want you just reading a lot of airy type ideas about time planning and then realizing that you would never put this stuff to use anyway.

LEARN THE THREE NEW STEPS TO ACTIVITY: BEGIN, CONTINUE AND COMPLETE

An important step in time planning is to realize that you get about 86,400 seconds in a day to finish what you started. Basically, time planning can be summarized in three easy words: *Begin, Continue, Complete.* How many things do you begin in a given day that you finally bring to completion? That cycle of activity is in direct proportion to how well your day is going to go. We hate incomplete activities. It drives us crazy. You energetic ones (during the morning hours) who start out like a bang and end like a bomb should keep in mind that trying to plan your day around too many things can really depress you. Why does it depress you? You and I hate not finishing things that we said we would. Self-esteem goes way down. One of the first things I would like to get across in this time planning discussion is *do what you can do and forget the rest.* Be realistic about what you can do. Why start out with a list as long as Christmas and find at the end of the day that you didn't even come close to wrapping things up?

SISTER MARY IGNATIUS SAYS: DO YOUR HOMEWORK THE NIGHT BEFORE

My best suggestion is to try what worked for me, especially if you are having a real problem being productive. I started planning my time the night before each new day. I would place my planner on the nightstand next to my bed and commit the things to writing that I needed to think about the next day. I did not fill the appointment calendar in at that point. My time planner has tomorrow's action lists in the back. I just write down the things I need to accomplish the following day on tomorrow's action list and move it forward to the next day. I place the list across from the appointment calendar section, knowing that the following day I will transfer important priorities and appointments from the list over to the calendar. You may ask, "Why wait until the next day?" Let's face it, salespeople have to be flexible when it comes to change. Let's say that I planned out my whole day the night before on an appointment calendar. The next morning I get up ready to go and suddenly I get a call and it's a hot connection. I am first and foremost a salesperson. Business connections should come first. Especially, if I have a day full of detail work, which I could squeeze in at another time. I want to stay flexible. How do I do this? Don't spend a lot of energy the night before setting priorities. Just write the list down fast on the action list and then go to sleep. By the way, you will sleep better because you are half committed now. You have written down your plan. The subconscious mind will work on your game plan for the next day, while you are asleep. I kid you not. If I forget to write this list before I go to bed, I feel like too much is up in the air and I find myself tossing and turning.

DON'T BE SO NOSEY WHEN YOU FIRST WAKE UP

I refuse to look at the time planner when I first wake up in the morning. Wait until you get yourself in a position where you can attack the day. Attacking the day means that you take the list that is written in the time planner and you begin to plug the appointments in across the page in the appointment section. The rest stays on the list. As you complete each appointment and article written on the adjoining list, you draw lines through the item. Why? Because you love to draw lines, you devil you! It tells you that something has been done and completed.

Check out the examples on the following pages from my personalized planner.

WHAT DAY IS TODAY?
TOUCH YOUR NOSE. PULL YOUR EAR

Another reason why it is not a good idea for you to look at the time planner first thing the next day is simple. It takes you out of the present moment. Too many people check their time planners out first thing in the morning, see what needs to be done for the day, then get depressed. Just looking at the planner in an area where you cannot do anything about the problem (when you first get out of bed in the morning) is not good.

Live in the "present moment." This is such a critical area in time planning. Women who have never worked and then suddenly are faced with having to get a job have a terrible time with this type of living. They are at the office physically, but mentally they are at the house with the kids. Guilt is a big part of being removed from the present moment. Our minds flash back to something we should have done. Perhaps we were short of temper with

TIME PLANNER
ORGANIZER

Order From:
Danielle Kennedy Productions
P.O. Box 4382
San Clemente, CA 92672 ● 714-498-8033

T.A.L.
TOMORROW'S ACTION LIST

▶DO DATE _____

MUST DO	DONE
	☐
	☐
	☐

PRIORITY

☐ _____ ☐

☐ _____ ☐

☐ _____ ☐

☐ _____ ☐

☐ _____ ☐

☐ _____ ☐

☐ _____ ☐

☐ _____ ☐

☐ _____ ☐

☐ _____ ☐

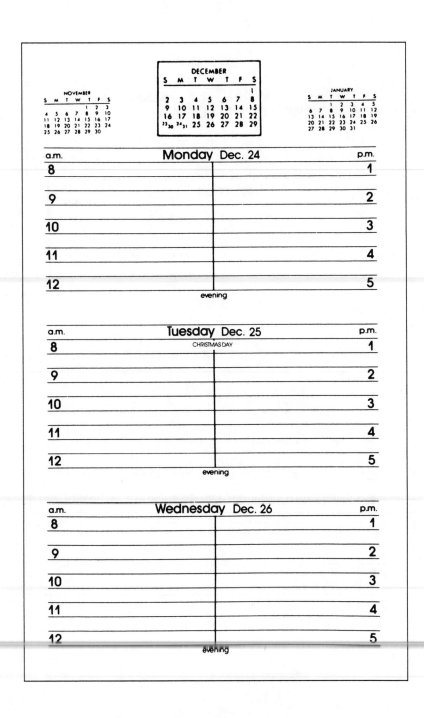

January 1985

TUES.	1	_____
WED.	2	_____
THUR.	3	_____
FRI.	4	_____
SAT.	5	_____
SUNDAY	6	_____
MON.	7	_____
TUES.	8	_____
WED.	9	_____
THUR.	10	_____
FRI.	11	_____
SAT.	12	_____
SUNDAY	13	_____
MON.	14	_____
TUES.	15	_____
WED.	16	_____
THUR.	17	_____
FRI.	18	_____
SAT.	19	_____
SUNDAY	20	_____
MON.	21	_____
TUES.	22	_____
WED.	23	_____
THUR.	24	_____
FRI.	25	_____
SAT.	26	_____
SUNDAY	27	_____
MON.	28	_____
TUES.	29	_____
WED.	30	_____
THUR.	31	_____

Names & Addresses	AREA CODE	Telephone

a child when we felt rushed for time. Now we wonder if we handled that situation correctly. Controlling the thought patterns is essential in living in the present.

What do you do when you find yourself being pulled off your purpose? Let's say this happens while you are at your desk doing some paperwork. Suddenly, you find the mind wandering and you are drifting. Ask yourself: "Am I bored? Would another time be better to do this project? Maybe I feel like going outside or just communicating and prospecting. Have I been sitting too long in one position? Then get up. Touch the wall. Touch your nose. Clean up the clutter. Is there a lot of clutter around you? Did you know that working in the midst of a lot of clutter is a reminder to you that you have not completed several things which you have begun? This makes you feel ridiculous and takes the mind out of the present and into your past losses and mistakes. Look at that piece of paper in front of you. Touch it. Can it be handled through a phone call right now? If it can, pick up the phone and immediately try to attack. Just attacking all the unfinished activities you have procrastinated about will bring you back into the present moment. Working one project on your desk (with no other physical distractions) can help. Try it.

CLEAN UP THE PAST. BURN IT NOW

The Chinese people had a custom. They would tie a rope from the ceiling to the floor at the beginning of the day. Then they would set the rope on fire with a match. By the end of the day, the rope was in ashes. It was a symbol of the past. And yet, we continue to lose ourselves and forget what the day is. Ask yourself right now: "What's today's date? Day of the week? Time?" Look at your hand. Touch the tip of your nose. Scratch somebody's back. Get into life.

A salesperson must really learn this art. Why? Because first and foremost they are commissioned. They usually do not receive a regular salary. And if they do, it usually is only a base salary and can be increased by productivity. All they have for tools of their trade is their mind and mouth. If the mind goes, then the mouth goes. I can detect from a salesperson's conversation if they are suffering from lack of the present. Rejection and loss pulls them into the past. They are at the office complaining about how slow things are. They are complaining about poor management or lack of this or that. They are chattering away the hours, trying to run from the biggest fact of all—they have ceased to begin, continue and complete a positive cycle of activity. You may ask, "What's the solution?" First answer is self-awareness.

PUBLIC ENEMY #1 IS YOU. INTERVIEW YOURSELF BARBARA WALTERS

In the area of self-awareness, let's begin by asking ourselves 13 questions. You and I are our own worst enemy when it comes to time. If I can get your heart jump started through these first 13 questions of self-awareness, maybe we can effect change. We have to look at what we do to hold ourself back. The first question fits in with our earlier discussion.

Question 1: *Am I hanging around the office and the quicksand crowd too much?* The quicksand crowd is the group who have nothing to do but talk on the phone, watch soap operas and criticize your efforts. "Are you crazy? You are going prospecting in the rain? No one does that. Stay here and eat a donut." They make you feel guilty for being productive. But we hang around them, often to soothe our wounds after rejection or to play victim. "The world is out to get me." They soothe you with, "Ain't it the truth?"

Question 2: *Am I refusing to do activities that I find distasteful?* A lot of people try to avoid pain. When we were little if we touched a hot stove, we got burnt. But the salesperson has to go out and learn. Just like the baby did. That means a few hot stoves and lumps on the head. Let's think about the baby for a minute. Remember when your kids were learning to walk? First they crawl. Then they creep. Suddenly, they are trying to pull themselves up around tables. Funny thing, but as soon as the table pulling starts, the cracks on the head begin. Here is baby trying like crazy to stand and wobble along. They dramatically pull themself up. Pow! They hit the side of the table and hit the floor. The poor thing is crying his or her eyes out. Mom and Dad watch and wonder how much longer this child is going to get knocked around. Notice, never at any given moment does that baby say, "Hey, look Mom or Dad, if I don't make it in the next thirty days, will you carry me for the rest of my life?"

Of course not. That kid is self-motivated and something keeps pushing baby on to the next move. Why? Because the kid doesn't know what to expect. There are no expectations there whatsoever. Baby is strictly in this to survive and move and no one at the office of babies clued him in. Picture that. Baby calls up his buddies and says, "What's with walking? How long will it take me? Do you know a short cut?" One of his buds says: "Lay low right now. Nobody is walking. It's stupid. You look stupid doing it. Plus there is a guy who can teach you to walk without any falls." But isn't this what salespeople do? Don't they try to find a way out of rejection and hurt? You have to take the "burn" to get the toned muscle. In exercise class my instructor is always yelling, "Go for the burn." I found out that the burn means that funny sensation in your stomach or leg after you have done 10, 15, or 20 situps or leg lifts. The moment you want to stop. But that is the exact moment that lactic acid (a chemical in the body) is released into the muscle and the toning action begins. To stop now would be a waste of exercise and give you no results. To stop at the customer who said you messed up is to never give yourself a chance to know who was around the corner dying for your services.

Question 3: *Am I putting off?* Maybe you have read that procrastination can cause heart attacks, depression and all kinds of physical ailments. Why? Because "what we resist, persists!" If you find yourself not doing the things you hate early in the morning, I will wager you that sometime through the day they will come back to haunt you. The complaint call is a perfect example. The customer got his furniture with a huge scratch on it. You keep saying, "I will call him. I will call him. Leave me alone with this. I will do it." And you do not do it. Next thing, you run into the guy at the local gas station and he gets you. Pins you right there. "You really are a terrible salesperson. You don't even return your calls." Guess who's got his head hanging for the rest of the day?

Now, that kind of stuff builds up. Can you imagine salespeople with a whole track record like that? They really start the relationship off great and end in disaster. They spend half their lives trying to cover up lies and mistakes. Their new mission in life is to look good in the midst of disaster. Why? Because they put off. They don't attack the plan every day. And believe me, that has sent many to an early grave. Not to mention the burnout they get right there on the job. Let's look at this fear again. What are we worried about? What are we putting off? Do you know the fear of telling the people the bad news (the delivery date is a week off; the merchandise has to be sent back) is usually a lot worse than actually delivering the bad news. Make up your mind that a customer is never going to pin you down again. When they call, call them right back. When you are trying to get them sold, call them early in the morning to show them you are on the job. When you have them sold, call them at off hours (like they do to you) to show them you are working the order. "Hi, Mary. Just wanted you to know I am hoping for an early June delivery date. I was on the phone with the manufacturer today." Throw 'em for a loop. Let them say: "Boy! That Joe is always one step ahead. Early up, late to bed. What a super salesperson."

Questions 4: *Am I avoiding risk?* Ask yourself: "Am I green and growing or ripe and rotten?" Are you one of those people that go for the comfort zone? Do you look for the warm fuzzies? Believe me, you do not belong in selling. If you love security, this is not the spot for you. The super naturals have really stretched their neck. The man that wrote the original script for the T.V. series *Mash* got something like 67 rejections. He finally said (before he tried the 68th), "If this doesn't fly, I am giving up." Of course, that one came in and he's been soaring with the eagles ever since.

I've tried like heck to avoid the risk too. In 1976, I was asked to speak before an association convention in northern California. I had established a track record in selling and now they wanted to hear how I did it. My first reaction to the invitation was "No way! I am not going to stand up and make a fool out of myself."

There were people around me who convinced me otherwise. The first half hour before the speech, I was in the bathroom. The last half hour after the speech, guess who was back in the bathroom. After my first full year in speaking, my company gave me a plaster of Paris toilet to symbolize my speaking career. Why? Because every time someone would ask me how my speech was, I would reply, "I was in the bathroom so much." Today people come up to me after a performance and they say, "I could never speak like that. It's so easy for you. Were you just born that way?" Nobody is born that way. We all have talents but without the risk and without the pain, we don't go from natural to super natural. And getting to super natural ain't easy. God doesn't come down and tap you with a wand. We are put here to take the risk. How boring, painful and meaningless life would be just sitting and avoiding any rejection at all costs.

Question 5: *Am I waiting around for things to get better?* Are you waiting out the bad economy? Me work now? Let's wait for ideal conditions. I met a lady on an airplane once. She told me she was married forty years. "The most miserable years of my life," she said. I looked at her and said, "How did you maintain in such misery for forty years?" She looked at me casually and said, "Oh, I haven't given up. Any day that man will change." Now that is what I call waiting and being persistent about it. This woman thinks she is perfect and the rest of the world is a mess. These types of people like to wait around for perfections. They do not look to themselves for more perfect solutions. It's always every-body else's fault. The office manager is disorganized. Their spouse is a slob. Their kids can't do anything right. There is no present moment, only the past to complain about and the future to wait out.

Question 6: *Am I giving in to mood swings?* Do you spend your time singing the blues and feeling either down and out or flying high. I am not talking about the truly depressed person. If you think you are, please call for help. I am talking about people like myself who pulled things like this when they first got into selling. I can remember that if I sold the customer something, I felt 11 feet tall. This one time, I swept into the office after the sale. I wrote my sale up on the sales board and strutted around like Miss

America. I would say things like, "Selling is so easy. I just can't understand how people can't sell, sell, sell." Then I would waltz home to the family and say, "Family, we are going to have a gourmet meal like you can't believe." They would secretly be thinking: "Thank God, we haven't eaten for days."

The next night at five o'clock, I sat in my depression cloak at the kitchen table. (The depression cloak is better known as my terry cloth robe with grape jelly and spaghetti sauce stains on the front.) I was crying my eyes out saying, "I am going to quit selling." The whole deal had fallen through and I was sick. Do you know what the worse part was? I had to go to the office and erase my name off that stupid board. When I put my name up there, no one was around. I take it off and the entire staff was glaring at me. And of course, everyone is so helpful at times like that. They stared at me and said, "Well, did you qualify the customer? Did you do this? Did you do that?" You'd like to belt those people. You are so depressed and they are helping you chew on the depression.

One of the reasons we get into the mood swings is expectations. We thought everyone would love us when we got into selling. Who do we think will be the first to come through with orders? You got it. Our best friends. They are the last to come through. They think we are stupid. "You sell computers? You don't even know how to add." Thanks friend, I needed that vote of confidence. Forget the friends. Go to the strangers and build your credibility. Quit expecting anything. Wake up each day and say, "Hey, I wonder what is going to happen today? I got a plan, but I wonder what interesting turn things will take?" Believe me it cuts down on the mood swings.

Question 7: *Am I refusing to let others do their jobs?* If we are involved in selling, there is a degree of competitiveness going on all around us. If we let it get to us, it can break our concentration, take us out of the present moment, and lose ground in the three circles of necessity. Here's usually what happens. New salespeople come into the selling scene. They are constantly being swayed and feel naive. They are also easily impressed. These new babies sit in an office working to get a foothold with major customers and find themselves getting nowhere fast. The climb to credibility with the customer takes time. Sitting across from these new salespeople is either million dollar Mary or Mike. This person is one of the high rollers in the office and has customers coming out of his or her ears. These new people get sidetracked and begin watching every move the million-dollar hero makes. Now this alone is not so bad, because after all, some of the best training I got as a new salesperson was from observing the pro in action. But on a particular day, when you are getting nowhere with a customer and a three-million-dollar hero gets a call and the order all in one day, it gets a bit too much to handle. We somehow try to figure out how to get into this successful world. We don't dare admit we are jealous because great salespeople are always happy for everyone. But we fake it and invite the pro to lunch. The pro naturally replies that he hasn't got a lot of time, but okay. "Gotta be back by 1:00 P.M. to take care of some new customers." We immediately reply, "Of course. No problem." (Inside we are wondering where they got these new customers.) Evil thoughts go through our minds like "I will take this bird to lunch and then get him loaded and hope that by 1:00 P.M. he is sleeping under his car, instead of hanging out with customers." But do we admit to any such thoughts? No way. A salesperson is always happy and never jealous. I told you early in the game that what we resist, persists. So, these nagging feelings keep lingering: "What am I doing wrong that they are doing right? Is he or she getting leads from an unknown source? Hey, I am better at people skills than this jerk. How do they get this business?" That's the first mistake. Why not admit to the jealousy so it will go away. Then take a realistic attitude and realize that you have done no "connection development" in the circle of necessity for over three months. You have been hanging on to some lost customer who doesn't really want to buy and it's kept you from going out among new prospects.

Why not pull out a note and jot this message down to the million-dollar hero: "Congratulations on your great month. I wish it was me! How do you do it? Sometime when you have a chance, could I pick your brain and ask you a few questions about prospecting? Meanwhile, I better get back at it and pull myself out of the intensive care unit of selling that I have straddled into." Much better way to go, wouldn't you say?

Question 8: *Am I talking too much?* A big time waster is our mouth. Do *you* find yourself going into the office and giving people around you a blow-by-blow description of the horrible things that have happened to you since midnight? You came home and found your spouse with another woman or man. The children were complaining because there was no bologna in the refrigerator. Suddenly, you realize that you are 15 hours late for an appointment and you are in deep trouble. As you rattle these facts off to whoever will listen, you have succeeded in interrupting someone else, as well as, yourself. Picture this. As you mention bologna, they remember they are out of bologna. They proceed to call home and find out that there is no bologna in their refrigerator. Your friend goes into a tailspin with you. I know I am exaggerating a bit, but can we stir things up if we want to? You betcha.

Try giving yourself a mental enema. That's where you drain everything out of your mind for thirty seconds and just try to stop the crazy thoughts. Sit there and stare into the darkness with your eyes closed. Get to the point where you can do a task and not be distracted until it is completed. No matter how crazy things get, keep your eyes on the ball. That's what the great athletes have to do. Crowds scream at Chris Evert Lloyd, Billie Jean and all the greats, but they just keep on keeping on. Concentration can be learned. But you must start slowly (try 30 seconds at a time) and build from there.

The other thing you have to learn is how to say no. Again, I think of my son Kevin, because of his dedication to gymnastics. This summer our whole family went to Idaho. Kevin was in the midst of learning several new tucks at the gym, which involved hours of concentration. He came to me before the vacation and asked if he could stay with his grandma and not go river rafting. He said he knew he had to concentrate and give up things if he wanted to succeed at what he was doing. He stayed behind. Saying no and not letting people sway you isn't easy. A lot of times you know best what you have to do to complete a goal, but people keep trying to talk you out of things. They won't let you get off the phone. They drop in unexpectedly and hang around. They try to use you to fill up their empty life. You may be called "cold and calculating" when you try to keep your purpose and goal in mind on a day-to-day basis. It's lonely and isolated to carve out a dream and stick to it. Sacrifices must be made. This is all part of the super natural plan of success.

Question 9: *Am I making snap or slow decisions?* Planning involves eliminating and including. This may also be called decision making. Some decisions we make very quickly. Others, we have to contemplate. I have noticed that the super natural stars do not major in the minors. You may say to them, "Where are you going for lunch?" They reply, "Well, I have ten minutes. I guess I will go across the street and grab a quick sandwich and then be back to do the paperwork sitting on my desk." The scared salespeople major in the minors. "Where should I go to lunch?" Decisions, decisions, decisions. They can take all day to order, once they finally make it to the restaurant. Same way with what to wear. The super natural star says, "Today I will wear the blue suit and white shirt with the red tie." When the super natural star goes on a trip, he or she will mentally pack beforehand and take ten minutes to do the physical part. The scared salespeople majoring in the minors will retort, "Gosh, what should I wear? The pink or the green or the gray. And, oh no, I just realized, I have nothing to wear. I haven't done a load in a year. Help! Help!"

Watch yourself and observe how long you are taking to decide to pick up the phone and call a few prospects, write some thank you notes or grab a sandwich. Speed up your reaction time. The super naturals do it every day. When major decisions come up, that's when we should back off a bit. Many times we are emotional when major decisions arrive and we need to wait until the heat of that emotion cools off. The employee is having a fight with his boss. The salesperson is arguing over a commission. A little physical fitness is the best thing to do at times like that when we reach a standoff with people. Then when the waves calm down, we can jump in again and make some important decisions.

Question 10: *Am I making unrealistic time estimates?* Right now stop reading this and make a real tight fist. Strain and push, even straining your facial muscles. Are you uptight doing this? Do you know people that run their day like this? They come charging into the office and they are fifteen minutes late for an appointment. They can't find their car keys. Everyone around them wonders when they will be leaving so they can get some work done. This comes from making an unrealistic list of things to be done for that day. It also comes from comparing yourself to others. You see people around you with a higher energy level and you say, "What's the matter with me?" Super naturals have one competitor—themselves and that is it.

Question 11: *Am I coping with change?* The only permanent state is change, so why fight it? So what, if you get a new boss? So what, if they make you move to a bigger or smaller office? So what, if your best friend moves on to another company? Nothing stays the same. But I know we fight change. In the last ten years, I went through more changes than most people do in a lifetime. Others in my generation have faced the same thing. Society is moving so fast. Families change and the expectations of women and men and their respective roles keep altering too. First, I went away to college. Then I got married and had five kids. Then I found myself in the selling field. I never had any enemies and suddenly, I was an enemy just because I might sell somebody something that the guy across from me thinks he has a right to sell. Then I went through a divorce. Then I was single and raising kids. Then I fell in love with one of my oldest and dearest of friends. Now we are combining friendship and love. Now we are getting married and parenting each other's offspring. Then I was writing books. Then I was trying to sell and still speak as a sales trainer. Then I moved. Then this and then that. I am a conservative midwest Catholic, who had a pretty sheltered upbringing. Then I began spinning. My dad, grandad and best girlfriend all died in a six-month period. Each change was painful. Some of the changes were excruciating. Some turned out to be real growth opportunities. I had to go through the dark tunnel and not know what the heck was going on for a while. I no longer knew how to talk to people I use to know real well. There were so many changes coming at me, I could have refused to get out of bed for a year.

Each change is a stretch. I love the onion analogy. As I change, I feel like an onion peeling off another layer, always getting closer to the core—which is me. The me that is me. Some will accept that me and others will choose not to accept. The beautiful thing about age and maturity is this: All of the above is okay. I don't have to have everybody's okay anymore. I do know who I am and what I like and don't like. I do know when I thrive best. I do know who I bring out the best in and who brings out the best in me. And I also know whom I drive nuts and vice versa. That's okay too.

I just have to flow with the changes, knowing that if I avoided and resisted this life I chose, I would be dead in a living body. It's called suppression. You see it in people who refuse to act. They prefer to stay in limbo. They don't want to say what they think. They prefer not to harm anyone. Of course, they get walked over in the process. But you find these people laughing on the outside and crying on the inside. They feel as if fate has dealt them a bad hand. How do you know if you fight change? Do you complain continually about every new idea implemented in your company before it is given a chance? Can you accept a new idea your boss wants you to try or do you continually say, "That's not the way we use to do it." Just observe *you* and see where you can stretch.

Questions 12: *Am I taking on too much?* Have you heard the expression "By the time that guy had made it, he had had it"? How many times have you seen people strive for power, money and success and die lonely and isolated? Happens all the time. Part of the super natural's secret is balance. They simply know when it's time to back off from work and smell the so-called roses. The new salespeople have quite a chore. They have to go out there and prove their credibility to the world. And anybody reading this might as well resign themselves to the fact that you have to work seven days a week and really hustle when you first try to build up credibility in your territory. But there comes a point when the family, and you for that matter, have had it. How much business do you want? How much time away from the loved ones are you going to take? You've made your mark and now it is time to shift gears. Shifting gears means finding some salesperson in your group that works like you. If you are a panicker, then hang around with panickers and ask them to mind your business while you are away. Delegate please. Hire a secretary or temporary help, especially during rush periods, when you just can't handle all the phone messages and paperwork. Don't be cheap and don't think you are the only one with all the answers. These folks that think no one can do their jobs like they can ought to try dying for a day. Stage a funeral. During the funeral, all your customers will be out buying something from another super star. Humbling, isn't it?

Included in all this planning and questioning, we have to say to ourselves, "How do I keep my super natural status in both selling and living?" Communicate along the way with the loved ones. Ask for their help. Tell them it is meaningless to make money without sharing it. Realize that sometimes the business has to wait. There are championship ball games, plays, graduations, birthdays, or just days when you have to be there. Other times, your job or the project must take precedence. That's when we say to the loved ones, "I am glad you enjoy this lifestyle. Now, in order for us to have this style of life, we all must cooperate. I have to complete this report, work with this customer, etc. I won't be around. Or I need quiet. So, please help out at home. Make your bed, your lunch. Don't complain. Don't ask for this and that and try to pull your load."

Teach the family not to ever *expect* things out of people, early in life. I see so many kids today who have no motivation. Why should they? They wear name brand $100 jeans, drive their own current year's model car (Dad bought it) and have plenty of money to either "veg out" or "zone out" with on drugs. "Is this all there is????" is the attitude they have about living. They see adults who strove night and day for power positions in their jobs. These adults gave them "everything they wanted." But was it everything? Sure they got the car and the designer jeans, but they never got the parent. They also never got self-motivated.

People ask me all the time about how my family likes my traveling. We were recently on a trip with an acquaintance who spent the whole time quizzing the kids about "Mom working and being away." The kids kept coming up to me and asking, "What is with this person? We keep telling him we think you do your job better than anyone and we are proud of you but he acts like we are being paid to say this." I was so proud of them. After all, they have given up time with me. But the difference is I have always kept my priorities fairly straight. I have the ability to "nicely" turn down time-wasting invitations in lieu of staying home with the kids. "I'd love to go the lunch, but I've got a commitment." I've told that to lonely customers for years. If I said, "The kids want me to drive them to the mall," I would have a rough time getting out of it. But "commitment" always sounded important. People have naturally thought I was *always* busy and working (nothing wrong with that getting out). But between you and me, I was probably fishing with my son or dancing in the family room with my daughter. "Commitment " is a great word to use on anybody but especially friends in the quicksand crowd.

The kids don't have everything they want and they work their tails off. My husband and I own Danielle Kennedy Productions and we work long hours. Our offices are connected to our house, so the kids see what's going on. But there comes a time when we stop and nothing comes between the walk, the talk, the swim, the run or the dinner together. A million-dollar contract couldn't change that. Recently I was asked to come to Canada a day early for an appearance on a big T.V. show. It was the same day as Kevin's gymnastic meet. The people up north kept saying, "But you are missing this chance." Five years ago I might have thought twice. But if you have been on one show, you've been on a thousand. I wouldn't trade anything for the thrill of watching my son or daughter perform. We will do the work we love to do and take plenty of time off and if it happens it happens. I hate myself when I am out of balance. And nobody needs to tell me when I am. I know and so do you. Quit fooling yourself. Work with one hundred percent concentration, but play that way too.

Question 13: *Am I motivated to sell?* Do you expect people to pump you up? Did you know that goals are an important part of motivation but long-term motivation comes from customer service? Listen to this. When I first began my selling career, money did motivate me. I would like to take it a step further. Family motivated me. I had a bunch of kids and I loved feeding them, dressing them and taking them places. Stupid me didn't know just how much money this was going to cost. One of the things I use to hate was going up to pay for the groceries and not having the necessary funds. So, when I went to work, my plan was to be able to have plenty of money to spend at the grocery store. As a matter of fact, I wanted to buy a freezer and load the darn thing up. I would just go open it up and check out all the goodies from time to time. The first six months that I was selling, I use to picture the Sears truck backing into my garage with a 22-cubic-foot freezer. Because I visualize my goals like a child does (see the picture in the mind before it happens), after I sold my first big one, I went and bought the freezer.

Then I started to want recognition. And believe me these are all *reasons*. There is nothing wrong with reasons. Especially, if they cannot harm anyone and every individual (both salesperson and customer) come out well. So, I started going to the awards breakfast each month for the people in my profession. These breakfasts would honor the outstanding people who sold more than anyone else in our association that month. I started banging out the business and hauling the trophies and plaques home. My picture started to appear in the paper. This was great. But I got saturated. I got so many awards for two or three years that the pressure was on night and day to sustain the power. Finally, I said there has GOT TO be more to this selling game than the recognition.

About this time, I became great friends with a couple who bought from me. A year later, they bought from me again, but the circumstances were quite unusual. He was a diabetic, had a diabetic attack and went blind in both eyes. He was collecting a ton of money and had some cash to invest. He called me up and said, "Danny, come over here and bring a contract. Just for today, pretend my eyes are your eyes and write up an agreement and go out and buy me an investment property." I was so sad to hear he had gone blind. I was overwhelmed that he trusted me so implicitly that he would let me handle everything sight unseen. That's when I got this choked up, overwhelming feeling inside that said, "They wouldn't do business with anyone but you." It got me. I couldn't stop crying. I realized that was the super natural high in this business. Being a star for certain people who think there is no one else close to you and your competence.

What we talked about earlier in this chapter all ties in with this last question of motivation. What have you begun, what have you continued, and what have you completed? I began a relationship with my blind friend and family and I completed it so well that the next time they trusted me enough to spend money for them. Did that motivate me more than a trophy? Did that motivate me more than a freezer? Oh, yes. Because I lived up to a promise. I said I would deliver the goods and I did. They liked what I did for them and now will do business again and tell others about me. This is what sustains the long term motivation.

STARTING AND COMPLETING: ARE YOU A BEGINNER, A MOVER OR AN ENDER?

The super natural plan involves handling a juggling act. We have to follow our intuition. At the same time, we have to get organized and follow some sort of a sketchy plan day by day. Intuition can't be emphasized enough. I can't tell you the number of times a customer's name would pop into my head that I should call. I may be driving down the street or eating in a restaurant. Often, I would stop what I was doing and whip out the organizer and look up their address and phone number. Then, I would call them and say, "I was just thinking about you and had to stop what I was doing." Often they would reply, "No kidding, we were just talking about you. We need to have you stop by and talk some business."

The plan must be structured to a degree. But, as you have probably picked up by now, there is a lot of trusting of self involved too. You know what you know. Don't ever let anybody put you into a position where you have second thoughts about what you know is right. How many times have we known what to do and then backed off because we got talked out of our idea? The super naturals know and trust themselves and their successful ways. They are aware of weaknesses they possess and have to eliminate. They plan on how to get where they want to go. Observe yourself. Trust your hunches. Follow your heart.

CHAPTER **3**

PICKING FRESH
PROSPECTS DAILY

Whenever I Feel Afraid, I Hold My Head Erect ♦ *Spit
It Out—Spunky New Scripts:*
  *Getting Past the Guard at the Gate; Research, Reach and
  Withdraw; Double Responsibility; What Do You Think?
  I've Got a Problem; Surveying the Neighborhood; Is This a
  Bad Time for You? I Don't Know If I Am Talking to the
  Right Person; The Survey; The Detective Script*
Make Many Mentors ♦ *Be Visible* ♦ *Don't Let It Get
You Down* ♦ *Territories Take Time* ♦ *Testify Please* ♦
Develop Writer's Cramp

Remember Dorothy and friends in the movie *The Wizard of Oz?*
Think back to how desperately they wanted to see the all powerful
Oz in person. He would solve all their problems. But they were
shaking in their boots. (Imagine us talking to the man in the ivory
tower.) How interesting we found it, once they confronted this
"power" person. The Wizard didn't have any answers that they
didn't already have and he was just as frightened to talk to them
as they were to confront him. After all, he always had his aides
around him to protect him and let him believe he was the strong
one. With defenses down and facing Dorothy and friends alone,
he was as scared as a helpless child.

I always think about us when I see or recall this story, the poor
salesperson wanting to get in and talk with the brass. We picture
some of these vice-presidents and presidents just as almighty as
the Wizard of Oz. There they are in their 20-floor office buildings
and we have to see "you know who" to get that order. In other
words, we have to prospect the brass and God knows we are

scared. Remember Richard Pryor, when he played the Oz, in the movie *The Wiz?* Once they finally got to him, he was hiding behind this huge prop that was supposed to symbolize the powerful Oz. He turned out to be a shivering kid in men's clothing. The fear you and I have of picking up the phone and going out in person to meet the decision makers is mostly irrational. Dorothy and friends thought the Wizard had *all* the answers. They looked to everyone but themselves to discover what they already had. Dorothy finally figured out that home wasn't too far away. It was right there inside of her. The tin man really did have a heart. The scarecrow most certainly had a brain. The dear lion was full of courage. But the smartest one of all was Toto, the dog. He always followed his instincts. Toto approached the Wizard.

WHENEVER I FEEL AFRAID, I HOLD MY HEAD ERECT

You too must follow your instincts and intuition when working with the world of people and prospects each day. Our biggest problem is the same as Dorothy and friends. We fear the first contact. We fear the first call, the first handshake. It seems the fear's impact depends on the so called power of the person. If I am talking to the guy at the corner gas station, no problem. What's to fear about him? But the vice-president of the muckety mucks is to be deeply feared.

Simple memories flash into my mind of fears like this. One time I was riding on an airplane, in the first class section of Delta airlines, returning from Texas. Who was sitting in front of me but Ed McMahon and wife. I just about died. Being such a star freak anyway, I thought I would flip right there. Scared to death, I wanted to go up to them and ask for an autograph. Knowing he started out as a salesperson, Danielle was dying to pick his brain. I was mad at myself already because I pictured riding the whole way home and not having the courage to say anything. Grabbing one of my workbooks from my seminar and a pen, I walked over to them and said: "I suppose you are always being bothered. But I am such a big fan. Would you please sign my book?"

That was the beginning of a three-and-a-half-hour conversation with two of the nicest people I have ever met—Ed and Victoria McMahon. I ended up sitting on the floor crosslegged while they told me about their family. We talked about Ed at age 19 selling pots and pans as a door to door salesperson in the midwest. It was the most thrilling plane ride for me yet. I kept asking them if I was interrupting and they asked me to stay. They told me how they met and fell in love. I discovered what a terrific relationship they had and also felt like I talked to two people who were un-affected by success except to make them appreciate life more. Can you imagine if I hadn't gone up and gotten that autograph? Two years later I did a commercial with Ed and he immediately re-membered our time together on the flight. Doing that commercial with a super star wasn't so bad. I was more relaxed because I knew he was a "real" genuine person.

The other problem we have in making a connection with people is worrying about what people think of us. Remember my story about my going prospecting in the rain, pregnant? Brother, was I afraid people would think I was slightly wacky. "A woman in her condition is doing that?" It turned out to be one of the most famous and legendary prospecting stories told in the sales field. There are even sarcastic jokers who have said to me, "When are you going to get pregnant again to promote yourself?"

SPIT IT OUT—SPUNKY NEW SCRIPTS

Let's talk prospecting. I am going to assume that you are going to try to do some of the things I suggest in the beginning with a certain amount of fear, but you will just learn to live with it until it passes. Okay? Okay. I am not just talking here about the new salespeople out there. I am also referring to the pros or the super natural kids, who want to stretch a bit and start working some bigger orders. The first thing we all have to do is learn to become fast script writers. I am a big believer in scripts. What do I mean by scripts? I am talking about what you will be saying to the customer on the phone, in their office, at home or during a presentation meeting. We are talking about the phrase, sentence or thought that catches their fancy long enough to give you a chance to break in and go for the performance.

You have got to become real fast on your feet. As a matter of fact take a public speaking course. Why? Because a salesperson is a public speaker with an audience of one instead of one thousand. Before you go out and try to wing the prospecting call, I would like you to take a blank cassette and a tape recorder and practice some of the scripts. Sit down alone in a room and listen to yourself deliver some of this stuff I will be giving you in this book. Talk the script. Put yourself in it.

Every once in a while I go down to our local public T.V. station and I help them raise money. When I go down there, we do a "live" show with people calling in to the station with donations. There are three of us positioned on the set. We each have a camera in front of us with a teleprompter in it. Have you seen your favorite T.V. personality or newsreporter looking at you directly on your screen, making you think they are just talking to you? Keep this in mind. They are reading a script. Now do I expect you to take a script out of your briefcase and start reading your "pitch"? (I hate that word!) Absolutely not. But I want you to outline the fine points of the scripts we will be doing in this book, customize them to yourself and learn them before you make the first contact. Guess what? Not only will you be prepared, but the preparation itself will help reduce the fear. I cannot tell you how important this is. One of the reasons I was so afraid to talk or approach people in the beginning was because I didn't feel justified in doing it. What reason did I have to talk to the prospect? You have to create reasons to call people to get the foot in the door. Your scripts must be informative, catchy and people arousing. Start talking to your first customer—you!

Check your delivery also. The words are fine but the music is better. Get in the habit of putting a mirror in front of you when practicing these scripts, particularly on the phone. Have you ever called a place of business and heard this? "Hello, my name is Mr. Grouch and I'm here to serve you." What you really feel like saying to this person is, "Are you sure you are not here to cuss me out for calling." This person hasn't plastered a smile on his face since 1942. These people are the type that say, "I love selling. I love collecting. I just hate people, that's all." None of my scripts will help this individual. So we are talking script plus delivery here.

The script must say lots of good things about your product. That means you must have tremendous product knowledge, even if you are new. If you are not so new, you better be sure your scripts are updated to include the latest changes and innovations in your industry. Review some of the pre-approach information outlined in chapter one. Go for the good research questions prior to the initial contact and watch that sinking feeling disappear.

Let's jump into some outstanding opening scripts that can be used on the telephone to aid us in getting our foot in the door. This fear that you have often comes out wrong and is misinterpreted when you make your phone calls. You say to yourself, "I have to sound like a big shot when I talk to Mr. High Brow's secretary." My husband Michael Craig is one of the best salespeople I have ever met. Thank God, because he is selling me everyday. He has told me time and time again: "Dan, there is no such thing as a superiority complex. People who come across that way are feeling inferior and this is their coverup to make them appear strong." That's why, when you and I get on the phone and have to "try" to impress somebody, it never works. People see through this shell.

The first phone script I would like you to work on is entitled **Getting Past the Guard at the Gate.** Let's assume that you are trying to get through to the senior vice president to get an appointment to present your wares. However, the secretary is the barracuda. She is there behind the door making sure calls and people don't waste Mr. High Brow's time. That is very efficient on her part. It's an important part of time planning. What you have to do is convince her that you are worth her boss's time. Don't ever try to get around her first. If you do not know her name when calling into the company ask the operator this:

"Yes, I am calling Mr. High Brow's office and his lovely secretary's name has slipped my mind. Can you tell me what it is and plug me into her?" She replies, *"Certainly, that's Polly Petit and I'll ring you*

through right now." "Mr. High Brow's office." You reply with, *"Yes Polly, my name is Danielle Kennedy and I have somewhat of a problem. (Don't pause.) Perhaps you can help me. I know how very busy Mr. High Brow is and you help him make the most of his moments all day. The last thing I want to do is waste any of his time or yours. But I have some outstanding information regarding a product and a service I provide that I think would make your department more profitable. What is the best way to handle discussing this with Mr. High Brow?"*

She may come back with, *"Well, what is this regarding?"* A lot of these administrative people do not like mystery and the "I can't tell you over the phone" type approaches. So, in order not to irritate this woman, we should try the following **Research, Reach and Withdraw Script.**

"Well Polly, I know there is nothing worse than a salesperson trying to get a choke hold on your day and using the mystery approach. I won't do that. As a matter of fact, I am not even sure our service will work (the take away). We provide paper airplanes (or whatever you do) for executives and their secretaries. We have found that a little playtime with paper in the middle of the day increases the productivity of the department from 3:00 to 5:00 P.M. Is this a product you could use or am I even talking to the right department head regarding this service?"

At Danielle Kennedy Productions often a press release or story comes out about me. We get a lot of calls. Some people who are interested in becoming speakers use this approach: *"I must talk to Ms. Kennedy. No one else will do."* This really incites Claudette, our coordinator. She handles our bookings and can give people more tips on speaking promotion than I can. But still they insist on talking to me directly. Claudette knows the number of calls I get from people who want to chat about being a speaker. It takes time away from my writing and family. It's not that we are not sincerely interested in helping others do well, but quite frankly, we are not a speaking bureau. If the party would realize the responsible position Claudette has in the company and direct some questions to her, she'd love to reply.

Do you realize the amount of time we waste talking to the wrong people regarding our services? We even make appointments using the mystery approach and get into the wrong department and find that our whole day has been wasted. Why try to be real cute and clever on the phone? We tie someone down and get in for the appointment and find out we are in the wrong place.

What happens if Polly says to you, *"Mail me a brochure. We don't do anything over the phone. We will review your material and get back to you."* What you are getting here is the bum's rush. Keep in mind some secretaries don't care how great your stuff is because they have overdosed on anybody talking to anyone and they ought to take a vacation. So here's how you handle this one.

"Well thanks Polly for telling me that. Please give me the name and address of who would be reviewing this material and I will send it out today." After you hang up, please sit down and write a good cover letter that specifically mentions Polly Petit. Compliment her in the letter (even if she was rude). Say something like this: *"Your secretary, Polly Petit, was so helpful to me on the phone today. I can see why you have her screening your calls and why your department is so effective. She suggested I send this information on to you regarding paper airplanes."* Complimenting her is a way to make sure the boss sees the letter (maybe).

Another good idea, when making initial phone contacts, is using a bit of humility and politness in the voice. When you finally reach the secretary or the person you wish to speak to, don't come across with: *"I am important so stop everything you are doing."* Don't you hate it when people call you with that attitude? Again, keep in mind that it's the old "superiority" attitude not working. Instead, say something like this:

"Yes Mr. Johnson, this is Danielle Kennedy with Paper Plane Products and I was wondering if I am catching you at a busy time? Perhaps we can talk later in the day?" Come right out and show them that their time is important to you. The key is to learn how to interrupt without irritating.

Let's jump into and practice some phone scripts. We have a name to use. A big source of business for me as a salesperson was to **leverage my way to the top with names.** A third party testimonial letter or the dropping of an influential name can break down the defense barrier and get you in the door fast, if used properly. Here we go: You have just been told by someone, who has done business with you in the past that a friend of this person may be interested in paper airplanes. Now, you can handle this two ways. The first way works great if you can get the person who is giving you the lead to put in a good word. Say to them,

"I have found, Sam, that if you call the friend who is interested in the product and you put in a good word, plus mention to that individual that I will be calling shortly, my chances of getting the appointment go much better. You can sell me better than I can. Would you mind calling Mr. High Brow (and tie them down to when they will do it) within the next hour and maybe give him some information about me and my work? Then tell him I will be calling him shortly."

What happens is this. The friend has a non-sales type conversation with the contact. They paint the contact a picture of you—the caring person. By the time you call, the bridge is half ready to cross. You may even tell the person who will be making the initial call what to say:

"Sam, thanks so much for talking to me and giving me this lead. Perhaps you could tell Mr. High Brow, when you call him, some of the things I did for you that you liked and even why you think my product is great. Also, if you feel I cared and was more interested in the service than the sale, please tell him that. It will ease his mind. I promise I will not let you down. If anything it will be more responsibility on my shoulders. I will have the responsibility of servicing Mr. High Brow and the responsibility of living up to the good reputation you have rumored about me." This is known as the **Double Responsibility Script.**

When you call the contact after Sam has called and set the mood, please use the **Double Responsibility Script** again.

"Hi Mr. High Brow. I feel I know you. I have heard so much about you from Sam. He told me I would be in real trouble, reputation-wise, if I didn't do a good job for you. That's in case you and I decided we can work together." (More take-away).

You must sit down after you get the appointment with Mr. High Brow and write him a thank you note and write Sam (who gave you the lead) a thank you note too. And remember—words work wonders. Try this in a short personal note: *"Dear Sam: Thanks to you the interview with your friend, Mr. High Brow, went great. I promise I won't let you down. I owe you a big steak dinner for this one."* Keep in mind that Sam feels like he has a mental stake in your success and if Mr. High Brow loves you, it makes him look good too. I cannot tell you the hundreds and hundreds of people who were out in every corner of my town working for me, when I was a new salesperson. I literally taught them how to spread good rumors about me. It comes across so much better when it isn't coming from you.

The other thing you must do is write the contact a note immediately after the call and later in the week after the appointment. After the call: *"Thanks Mr. High Brow for taking the time to talk to me. It was a privilege and I promise, when we get together on Thursday at 2:00 P.M. (confirming the appointment), it will be time well spent. Don't forget, I have to let Sam know I am doing a good job too. He said the last thing he needs is you upset with him for sending a real incompetent salesperson to your door. See you soon."* Then write a note after the appointment confirming the next move and thanking him again.

Let's say you are dealing with a person who will not make the final decision regarding your product. You present your product to them. Then they review and research whether it will fit into their company and they present it to the decision makers. The whole time that you are working with assistants, I want you to really get that person on your side. As they learn about your product and you have meetings with this person, reassure them constantly that they are doing a great job. This is your liason to the head banana.

Up until this point, we have been discussing scripts to get in the door with or without a contact. What about all my friends out there in direct selling, who have to make cold calls to scan the area everyday for new business. Some of you are saying to yourself, "I never know what to say. Give me something to say." Try some of these scripts for the typical cold call.

"Hi, this is Danielle Kennedy with Paper Planes, Inc. What Do You Think?" For a few seconds there is no reply. Then you will get this: *"What are you talking about?"* You come back with: *"What do you think about our reputation as a company in the community? Have you noticed our newspaper ads? Has anyone in your household flown one of our paper airplanes?"*

The response is great. No one asks nor cares about another's opinion anymore. Behind many a closed front door, there is a group of people dying to express their opinion. Many times, women can't get anyone to listen to them at home. The kids hear what they want to hear, the spouse is preoccupied and now someone is asking her opinion and she is loving it. I have received some excellent input from this script. For instance, one time I got a great advertising idea from one of the ladies I was making a What Do You Think? call to. She said.

"Of course I know who you and your company are. You people serviced the family down the street with your product and did a great job. We also enjoy your ads in the paper. I thought of a clever one you could do for Easter. . . ."

Mayor Ed Koch of New York was seen on the T.V. program "20–20" recently. He used a similar script. He and Barbara Walters went down into the neighborhood of New York and he saw people standing on sidewalks and hanging out their windows. He would just go up to them and say, "How am I doing?" I saw that and figured I wasn't all wrong.   Sometimes these calls don't go all that well. Don't be discouraged. Count on some calls going sour. It's only natural. You are dealing with large numbers of people when you sell and if you hide in the closet, nothing will happen. Of course, you won't get any problems, but you won't have any orders either. We have to be able to take the good with the bad. If we have complainers, we must tell them we appreciate the input and we are striving to do better. Institutions are imperfect and mistakes occur. Ask them for a suggestion. A constructive suggestion. Don't be alarmed by complaints. If they are rude to you just comment, *"I didn't mean to ruin your day. Thank you very much."* Then hang up.

You can also use the **What Do You Think? Script** for a reason. Say your company has an ad campaign going on with lots of T.V. or newspaper advertising right now. This can make a perfect excuse for a call:

"Hi, this is Danny Kennedy with Paper Products, Inc. What do you think of our advertising campaign for the new models?" Your company loves the idea of you following up with phone calls and notes

after they spend a great deal of money advertising their product.

Try the **I've Got A Problem Script** with past satisfied customers. Maybe you are scanning for new leads. Call the old customer and say,

"Hi Mitch, this is Danny Kennedy with Paper Products, Inc. (Unless you feel mentioning the company name is too formal.) *I've got a problem."* (Pause). He replies: *"What's up Danny?"* I reply, *"Well you have given me a lot of business in the past and hopefully you are satisfied with our dealings together. Now, I'm asking your help. My problem is I need to meet more people who need these great services (products). Can you refer me to any of your friends or relatives and help me with this problem?"* This is such fun. Why? Because they love you, have a stake in your success and want to see you do well. Ask. Ask. Ask. It never hurts.

This next script is kind of casual. The purpose is to check on the pulse in your area and get a feel for the competition. It's great for my direct sales people. Here goes:

"Hi. I'm Danny Kennedy, your local _____girl. **I Am Surveying the Neighborhood** *to see what my competition is and to find out if it gives you the same benefits that my product will. What type of vacuum system do you presently use in your home?"*

Keep in mind this script has to be used with a lot of people. You are going to get a lot of turndowns. Look to one or two leads per 100 calls on this. But one call, one appointment, thus one sale, can make all the difference in the world. Remember, we are scanning and we have to do a lot of it and not take rejection personally.

Always soften the intrusion on these calls when you get a positive response. Say you ask them about the system they now use in their home. They give you an answer and don't hang up. Immediately use the script (one similar to the one you used with the busy executive). *"Is This a Bad Time for You? I can call at a more convenient time, but I do want to get your opinion on something."* Pause and wait for response.

A script that my husband Michael uses to cold call for job prospects for me is a winner. It is called **The I Don't Know If I Am Talking to the Right Person Script.** It is really a powerful one for selling any kind of product or service to companies or people.

If you can get your hands on good mailing lists (the kind with up to date names, addresses and titles) this can work like a charm. One of the problems we face are mailouts going to people who either do not handle the decision we need handled or people no longer employed at that particular company. If you even want to update your mailing list, this script will do that for you too. Watch:

"Hi, this is Michael Craig with Danielle Kennedy Productions (this should be delivered with a bit of tongue in cheek humor) *and I am confused and don't really know if I am speaking to the right person or not."* When you practice it, sound a little stupid. (People prefer stupid to cocky.) Usually Michael will get a neat response like, *"I don't know if you are either, but try me."* Then Michael will proceed with: *"Well, I represent a woman lecturer named Danielle Kennedy. Do you get involved in booking speakers for programs for your company?"* You could change that to: *"I represent Paper Planes, Inc. We have some of the most colorful models out there but why waste your time if your company has no use for them. Do you, by any chance, get involved in paper planes?"*

If that organization has no use at all for your product, then there is no point in continuing the conversation any longer than it takes to politely end it. If your list is good, quite a few of these conversations will turn up companies who do use speakers or paper planes. You will then be able to ask questions that lead you directly to knowing whether you should do the following:

1. Fly out to see them at once.
2. Send them a brochure.
3. Send them a quotation.
4. Design a special paper plane or presentation for them.
5. Put a card about them in your tickler file to call at a specific time in the future.
6. Contact someone else in that organization for an appointment.
7. Forget about them because paper planes don't fly in their group.

Keep in mind that if you get any kind of positive response, you must SEND THE THANK YOU NOTE AT ONCE. Say something like, "I didn't know who I was talking to when I started out, but it sure turned out to be a nice person." Perhaps they couldn't help you, except to put you directly in touch with the office that handles paper planes. They even gave you a tip off on the decision maker and another interesting tid bit. "O'Brien hates salespeople but I know his supply is running low so let me call up there and talk to Sherry and tell her what's cooking." This happens to us so much when we do not come across as big shots with this **Help . . . I Don't Know Script.**

So far we have been discussing strictly telephone warmup scripts. What about face to face methods. Some of you say, "I hate it Danny. I do not like direct canvassing at homes, office buildings or anywhere." I think you are closing a big door of opportunity here that you should consider opening. There is a time and place in your life for three types of prospecting: Ears, Feet and Hands (note writing). You must use writing, listening, talking and walking skills. The other day I heard Tom Hopkins on the telephone. He is probably the foremost sales trainer in the nation today. He gets on the platform and spellbinds an audience. He is still prospecting, though. Tom was talking to a decision maker regarding a series of speeches he would possibly be delivering to this man's company. The man said, *"Perhaps we can get together sometime. I would like to meet you in person."* Tom immediately responded with: *"How about this afternoon? I can change my schedule, if you can fit me in."* The man was amazed with the quick reaction. He, being caught off guard, said, *"Sure. What time? Two or three?"* Tom took it from there.

A good prospector knows when to jump on opportunity and when to back off. It reminds me of picking fresh fruit off a tree. Some peaches just aren't ready so you go to the next branch. You keep scanning. You may come back later to that one, but you don't pick it just yet. Pick the prospects that want to be picked and leave the rest of them alone. We sometimes concentrate too much on unripened prospects.

More than likely you are now thinking: "Is she going to give me some face to face scripts to practice?" You betcha! I expect you to be completely prepared at the door of wherever you find yourself. You can use the same scripts I gave you for the telephones when you are out on face to face calls as well. But here are some more:

The Survey Script. *"Hi, I am Danny with Paper Planes, Inc. I hope I am not catching you at a bad time. If I am, perhaps we could arrange an appointment. I am conducting a survey and need some questions answered regarding my product and the needs of your company."* Again this one will have to be delivered to a lot of folks to get an appointment. If you just get the chance to come back with a set appointment at this point, I want you to consider that a real win. At least you didn't get a no.

Keep in mind, if you are a territorial salesperson (such as a pharmaceutical representative calling on doctors), the first step is to just get your foot in the door. You need to get identified. You need to build up credibility. This takes time. So, when first working the territory by foot, the survey can work wonders. Also, if you have giveaways, please use them. Samples of your products, scratch pads, rain hats for girls in the offices, calendars, appointment books or whatever. Stuff that has your name and picture really work. When I first started my sales career, I use to give away scratch pads with my photo on it. It also had my name and company plus the phone number and address of that company. Imprinted on the scratch pad were emergency phone numbers of fire, police and local hospital. People kept them handy by their phones, tacked on to their refrigerators or just about anywhere. I often would go into the grocery store and find a sheet or two balled up in a grocery cart with a list of items to buy at the market. People love "free" items.

Andreino is the owner of one of the finest Italian restaurants in the U.S.—"Andreino's." We had dinner there one New Year's Eve. Andreino is always working the crowd. He's got the business but he's prospecting for more repeat business. "How's the dressing tonight? Is everything to your satisfaction?" He also used giveaways that New Year's Eve. As we left the restaurant full and happy, he handed me three free samples of expensive perfume. What a charmer!

Here's another good one—**The Detective Script.** Let's say you have some credibility with the people in your territory now. You are at least getting a "Hi Mike" when you stop by. The next step in foot prospecting is trying to pinpoint certain people in your territory who have some clout. They know a lot of folks and seem to be not nosey, but a bit "curious." You find yourself chatting with them a little longer than some of your other calls because they always seem to know what is happening. Try this:

"You know George, you seem to really have a handle on your business and what goes on in the industry. Can I ask a favor (don't pause)? Could you keep your ear open for information leading to people who may be in need of my services? I'd love to take you to lunch and discuss some ideas I have." They like lunches, love to talk and probably will fill you with lots of good leads and information. Always reward that person with a lot of praise, thank yous and even little gifts, if appropriate.

MAKE MANY MENTORS

Some people in high positions would be insulted if you sent a gift. They have "made it," so to speak, and like the idea of helping this young salesperson climb to the top. That alone is thanks enough for them. In my business, we call this "mentorship." Marilyn Van Derbur, a former Miss America and one of the greatest motivational speakers, says, "There isn't anyone who has achieved any goal who hasn't had a mentor." I think salespeople often forget that they must find their mentors out in the field during their prospecting sessions and really work those mentors. Of course, I feel we have an obligation to repay that debt some day when we in turn "make it." Then it is time to help new fresh talent up the same ladder we stretched for in the beginning. Make sure it's "motivated," fresh, new talent. Sometimes we serve as mentors for people who only think they want to do it, but are unwilling to pay the price. They are merely *expecting* handouts and shortcuts.

When we are building identification, in the early stages of foot prospecting, we should have our eyes open for possible mentors. But it isn't until the sense of belonging, feeling comfortable and fairly credible comes into play that we ask the mentor for the help. During this period of progress, keep in mind that if you bug people too much and you get to be known as the town "pest," you could seriously hurt your chances of total acceptance with the crowd.

BE VISIBLE

If you are in direct sales and extremely visible to the public, drive the area a lot without actually talking to anyone. I use to do this on Saturdays around 1:OO P.M. People are usually out mowing their lawns. Maybe they are washing their car. You wave. Seeing you reminds them that they are out of their supply of cold cream, cleaning liquid or whatever you sell. You are in the right place at the right time. I cannot emphasize enough, once you are known, how truly critical it is that you remain *visible*. People do a lot of things on impulse. If you are there, things can happen to you. If you are not, and someone else is, you lose. Don't limit this idea to the door to door salesperson. If you call on banks or major corporations, the same principle holds true. Seeing is always believing.

DON'T LET IT GET YOU DOWN

What happens if you are having a horrible day? Every prospector who goes out on foot and puts himself or herself in a vulnerable position with the public is going to have some of those days. How well I remember going out one rainy day to a lady's house and watching her open the door in her bedroom slippers and robe. The cat jumped out the door and ran up the slope behind her house. It was full of mud and ground cover called ice plant. In California that is the mushy stuff that has water inside that splats all over. She went charging up the hill to get the cat. I stood there frozen to the ground thinking, "Oh no! Help." She came back down the hill with the cat all right. She was on her back side and swearing vulgarities. "You—-salespeople. No I don't want to buy a mop, move or fly your stupid paper airplanes. Get out of my life." Slam. The door registered closed in my face. I walked away thinking, "Why me, Lord? Give me a secure desk job and a time clock and let me live in peace happily ever after." Usually on days like that, you just go home and feel sorry for yourself.

That day I was driving in my car and landed on a street of an old client that I dearly loved. I walked up to the door and she answered. I said, "Julie, do you still love me? Do you think I am a good salesperson or do you hate the air I breathe?" She laughed so hard that it got me laughing. "Of course we love you," she said. "Now come on in. I have to show you how we fixed up our family room. Oh and come to think of it we were about to call you. I think we have a good prospect for you." What a great way to end a miserable day.

TERRITORIES TAKE TIME

I like to tell salespeople that it will probably take them a couple of years to build up their credibility in a territory. If you are part of a big corporation and you've just been given the cherry territory that's one thing, but if you are like most new salespeople, you will have to start from scratch. During this period of building, listen like crazy for tips and leads. Take advice from other salespeople in your firm who are now where you want to be. Watching the winners is the best kind of training.

During the second year of building, you will notice you are forming an army of supporters. Please stay humble. Remember who the mentors are and constantly tell them, "I owe this all to you." Do a lot of nice things for the mentors to let them know you so appreciate them getting you to this stage of development. People who have captured their territories throw great Christmas parties for their customers. They remember offbeat things no one else does (the day they had their first sailing lesson or sunk the Hobie Cat). Actually, they have great rapport with the whole family, especially kids. ("Hey Mom, Dean's on the phone. Tell him about the guy up the street who needs a new paper plane.") I found that kids helped me as much as their parents did. When you get involved with your customers, you know all about them. Read the interview chapter and realize that asking questions is a critical part of what a super natural does. We are not just talking about sales here. We are talking about building lifetime relationships with people that think you are honest and have a terrific product. If you should ever leave your territory, it should be bequested to another super natural who uses the same style you do. This has been built up with kid gloves and deserves special treatment.

TESTIFY PLEASE

Leveraging with names is a good move in the high performance stages of prospecting. Asking the third party to call the lead first is something you can get away with easily, when you have credibility in your industry. I also think testimonial letters are a must. As you build your reputation in your field, get the excited customers to write a formal testimonial letter. Start a file of all these letters. Then, whether you are prospecting by mail or in person, use a copy of the letter in a visual presentation. Or send it by mail with a cover letter. People are sometimes shy about doing this. Try this script:

"I can't tell you how glad I am that you are pleased with my service. **I Need to Ask You a Special Favor** *that would really aid me in my career. Could you possibly write a letter of testimony, sharing some of the specific things you felt good about when we worked together? People feel so much better buying something from someone who has earned praise from the customers."*

I have never gotten a no on that one. What I do is ask for the letter after I have delivered the service and they are especially pleased. If I am in Jacksonville, Florida, and I have just finished a presentation and the mood is high, I automatically get ready to ask. And I don't feel embarrassed. Number one, it is obvious they liked what I did. (If it isn't don't ask. I have had those kind of days, believe me.) I usually am taken out to dinner by the person who hired me. Sometimes they take me to the airport. I wait until we are alone and they plant some praise on me. "Danny you did a great job. You are making me look great for bringing you in." Perfect. I come back with, "Boy, am I glad to hear that. There is nothing worse than a person having to face a crowd because they brought in a bad speaker. I sure wouldn't want to make you or myself look bad. A lot of times people who have never heard me worry that they could be making a bad decision for their upcoming program. You could help me tremendously by taking a few extra minutes next week and possibly writing a testimonial letter to me." They always say, "No problem."

Sometimes people forget to write the letter. My secretary and I have now figured a way to handle that. Write a trusty thank you note and do a P.S. like this: "By the way, I know how busy you are but if you get a chance pop off a testimonial letter. It really helps me go forward and do more programs." Works like a charm every time. Don't be afraid to ask when you earn the right to do so.

DEVELOP WRITER'S CRAMP

So much of successful prospecting is just having the ability to communicate. So far, we have been talking about vocal communication by telephone or in person. But I cannot emphasize enough the importance of the fine art of writing. To be able to pick up a pen several times a day and write not only a thank you note but a "thinking of you" note makes a lot of sense. Here are some handy tips regarding prospecting by mail:

♦ Hand address every prospecting piece that you mail out.

♦ Use plain envelopes instead of printed company envelopes. Do not use a rubber stamp in the corner; handwrite your return address too.

Mass mailing:

♦ Carefully select your list from sources that are both recent and local. Old names are bad names for prospecting.

♦ Make your message short, friendly and readable.

♦ Follow up every prospecting card and letter you send with a phone call or a personal visit. This is vital. Do it as soon as possible after your mailing gets there.

I have seen people spend an awful lot of money on bulk mailings and leave town the day the piece hits the prospect's door. It is so ridiculous to try to use the mail without a followup phone call script. Try this:

"Hi Mr. Chester, this is Danny Kennedy from Paper Planes, Inc. Did you receive the information I sent you regarding our new models? (Don't pause.) *Or is this something that is throwaway mail to you?"* (Said with a bit of humor, not sarcasm.) You might add, *"So much of what we receive in the mail we just throw away. I wanted to make sure you didn't feel that way about this information."*

It is important when prospecting to give the customers you are working with that "you know what it is like to be in their shoes" attitude. If you are interrupting the executive, you say, "I know people hate to be interrupted." If it's the housewife at the door, "I hope you aren't feeding the baby," (if that's an obvious scene in that house). By saying what they are thinking, it takes away some of the irritation on the interruption.

The best hours to do all types of prospecting are an important part of this chapter. For instance, people who are into direct sales should keep in mind that researching their neighborhood is the best way to find out when most people are home. Today's society is filled with two career couples. So many times calling or appearing in the middle of the day makes no sense at all. If you fly from state to state handling a territory, your secretary will need to get your customer's business and personal itineraries. Learning when people vacation regularly each year, go to quarterly meetings or just spend a day a week outside of their office is important information to know. Direct sales people I work with say that Saturday is a pretty great day to visit the neighborhoods. Most people are out in the middle of the afternoon raking leaves, washing cars and generally doing chores in a relaxed mood.

Calling people during the dinner hours isn't too smart. Why not call between the hours of 7:00 and 8:30 P.M. That way dinner should be over and it isn't time to retire yet. Newspapers tell us that Wednesday and Sunday are the two biggest days of the week for newspaper reading around the country. Take advantage of people being in a more curious buying mood on these two days. When they read the newspapers, they are often looking for bargains and you may call them at just the right time.

Timing is something that you are going to have to work on. Following your intuition is smart if you are in selling. When a prospect's name pops into your head, pick up the phone and make the call or drop in if appropriate. Many times we start to call and freeze on the spot. Making that call or stepping out of the office at the right time to knock, walk and talk is the first step. You may not have the script perfect, but you are out there. And the big difference between the prospector and the lazy bones is just the act of doing it.

The super naturals all started out not knowing exactly what to do or say. They began creating some spontaneous scripts, recording them in their memory and then on paper. They received good reinforcement when the customer gave them excellent feedback. Therefore, every time the opportunity arises again, they use the script with a new person. Just go pick those cherries daily. There are so few who are, believe me.

CHAPTER 4

THE HOMEGROWN
BRAND OF INTERVIEW

I admire Barbara Walters so much. She asks all the right questions—just naturally. She asks the kind of questions that everyone watching secretly wishes they could ask if they had this very same person in their living room. I will never forget one time when she was interviewing Burt Reynolds. Barbara asked him about his breakup with Sally Field. She prefaced a personal question with a factual statement. She reminded him of the time he mentioned he'd love to spend the rest of his life making movies with Sally. And of course, he immediately searched his mind and wondered if this was true. Did he say that? Then when he remembered that he did, he probably told himself, "Gosh has Barbara got a good memory. She is actually quoting me correctly." This immediately gave Barbara credibility in his and the audience's eyes. Just watch those defense barriers come down. The whole time she did not pause once. She hit him with the statement then wham—got him with the question.

Now will someone please tell me who's one of the greatest salesladies in the world? You got it. Barbara Walters. When I call her an ABC correspondent, anchorwoman or news reporter, people are impressed. When I say she can sell, you go "yuk." Please give credit where credit is due. She can sell, ladies and gentlemen. What can she sell? Her questions and her ability to get answers. Plus she can sell herself into the living room of the celebrity in the first place. That is a feat in itself. Take Paul Newman for instance. He *loves* his privacy. Makes no bones about it. Rarely does interviews. Who wows her way into Paul Newman's living room? You got it. Barbara Walters.

Barbara Walters makes interviewing look so easy. Most of the a la naturals are the same way. You feel like you've known them your whole life. But that confidence and naturalness comes from homework, study and preparation. That's why we inserted pre-approach information earlier in this book. The following story is a perfect example of what happens to an interview, then consequently a future sale, without preparation. Not so long ago, Mike and I were in the market for a new king-sized bed, mattress, down pillows and all the trimmings for our new bedroom. Splashed all over the newspaper were "white sales" at some classy department stores. We are the perfect example of two people who didn't need to be sold again. First it was the car, now the bed. This time we didn't meet up with a sarcastic liar. Instead, we walked into the hands of an ill-prepared, very new saleslady. She was honest but dumb. I know I was dumb too, but I knew it and locked myself in bathrooms to try and prepare myself before the encounter. She not only lost her store a $1,000 sale, but acted like it wasn't her fault. It was this kind of attitude—"I can't help myself. I'm new."

We asked her about the specially priced mattress and box spring. She told us she didn't know where they were. Finally, I suggested she ask a cohort where they were. She was told that they weren't available at that store. Okay, what about the down pillows? She walked us over to the pillow section. Mike said, "We want the best down feather pillows you have." Believe me folks, there was no sale involved here! She couldn't even take an order. "Let's see," she said, "I'm not sure what is down and what isn't." We all fumbled through bins and bins of pillows. This went on for minutes and she kept letting people interrupt her time with us. Finally, we happened on to two big down pillows (we brought in some of her other teammates for assistance) and staggered out of there exhausted. There was no approach behavior. There was no questions or mini interviewing on her part, just confusion and frustration. Meanwhile, this major store had spent hundreds of thousands of dollars on expensive advertising with no backup. Gosh, I hope some of those people read this book.

Let's replay the scene and show what could have happened. Then we will dissect the interview through the rest of this chapter and show you how it's done. We walked into the bedding department on this particular day and there were three ladies working. There was plenty of help. The new salesgal could have greeted us and said, "Thanks for stopping by. Are you in the market for some bedding or just looking?" (Keep in mind people who *want* to buy are just dying for some help. The fast sale is the person who usually isn't a looker or a shopper. They know what they want and love someone who reacts as fast as they do. Most of the time the stores cater to the lookers because they mistake the real buyer for the impatient intruder.) With great relief, we would have said, "Oh yes. We need a king size bed and mattress (on sale), some down pillows and sheets." She would have responded with, "That ad you saw for the mattress and box spring is only available at our Newport store, but I can call and have one held for you or perhaps we can ship it directly to your home."

She would have paused for a response. And then with confidence, the salesgirl would have taken us directly to the pillows and sheets and pointed out our options, knowing exactly where each item was. She could have continued asking us questions. "What color room are you doing? Do you have a dust ruffle and coverlet? Tell me about colors you enjoy. We have a fine selection of colors. Peaches, pinks or stripes. I'll show you some of the favorites and see what we can fit in for you." We would have felt like we had died and gone to heaven.

The interview feels good to you. It feels good to the buyer. It's a combination of asking questions and visually picturing in your mind's eye your product(s) and where the need of the buyer and your product could fit together. It's like the solving of a riddle or fitting the pieces together of a puzzle. The whole purpose is to ask a question out loud, and then (quietly to yourself) match up an answer to that need of the buyer. Salesperson says to customer, "Are you in the market for bedding?" They say, "Mattress and box spring." You think to yourself, "I don't have any here. I can send them to the other store. Call first, show a photo, or have them test a twin bed we have in stock for firmness and then write up an order and have it shipped direct." Do you see how you need to know what store they have them at, if there is a twin in this store that's the same quality and where the catalogue is to demonstrate a picture? Fast, swift reactions. A prepared person and environment. Lots of homework goes on behind the scenes. Thank you nuns all over Chicago, who taught me never to be caught with my guard down before a test or a spelling bee. The old homework paid off, sisters!

THE TURTLE THEORY

Sometimes a customer comes to you like a turtle in a shell. Picture this: You greet the people. They've got their arms crossed. There are no smiles. The message that's coming across is "A salesperson. Yuk. Trying to sell me something I'm not sure I want. I'm just looking." Just like the turtle, the customer refuses to come out of it's shell. You wouldn't think of taking that turtle's head and pulling it out. Same deal with the customer. Don't pull! We use the same coaxing techniques on the person that we do with the turtle. If there is something around to interest the turtle, believe me he will stick his head out. If not, he'll keep moving slowly in another direction. Don't get too excited either. If you act like this is the first breathing soul you've seen in 20 years, they will do a disappearing act. Turtles and customers do better with slow, easy starts.

EYE TO EYE CONTACT

Keep good eye contact even if they aren't; don't you scan the room nervously. Set your eyes on their eyeballs. If there is a husband and wife *divide* the eye contact up evenly between the two of them. What if you are a saleslady? What if you are a "10"? For crying out loud don't just look at the man! She'll want to make a beeline for the door, screaming, "I hate this woman. I hate her." I say this because I train thousands of women (and men) and believe me, some of you are knockouts. You often come up to me and say, "Danny, why do men I'm working with seem to be making passes at me?" My first question is Why is the question even coming up? Get your mind on business and *ignore* the pass. And next, don't keep giving *him* all the eye contact. She's your ally too. If you want to run for flirt of the year, get out of selling and try for Miss America.

Now guys, the same goes for you. Divide the eye's action. Don't talk "with the boys," when you sell. Look at the little lady (no I don't mean flirt with her) and include her in the questions. She may hold the purse strings. While you are in the corner talking things over with the man of the house, she may be thinking, "Little does this creep know, the checkbook is in my purse."

If you've ever gone to a cocktail party and felt left out in a group discussion, the above points should come through loud and clear. There you are, standing in a group and one person is monopolizing the conversation. The monopolizer is just looking at one set of eyes. As a matter of fact, the rest of us might as well not even be there. If you are new to the group at this party, you feel like a total idiot. You don't know what to say for fear it will be stupid, especially because the two that are giving each other eye contact and conversation make everyone feel that they are the only ones "with it." So divide the eye contact up evenly between all parties.

DOES THE BODY HAVE A LANGUAGE?

Sounds dumb, but yes. I use to die when I'd hear about seminars and books written about body language. How ridiculous, I'd think. I don't know one body that speaks a word. But after you get involved with the customer in the selling scene, you do notice things. Things like folded arms. Things like people stepping back when you step toward them. Or how about touching? Some men definitely give saleswomen the idea that they do not want to shake their hands. Or how about when you touch a customer on the arm with a friendly gesture in mind early in the confrontation? Suddenly, you get the distinct idea that they feel that's "too personal," too soon. So you go back one step and withdraw. If I see a customer acting cool, I'll keep my distance. Don't touch them, if you sense it's uncomfortable for them. As you begin to prove your competency and sensitivity to their needs, that alone will stand to build a close professional relationship. Someday they'll be giving you a big hug because they are pleased with the great job you've done for them. Move in slow. People are funny about strangers invading their territories.

Some of you may say, "Why can't people be more open and touching?" Leo Buscaglia is a famous lecturer, author and "hugger." He hugs thousands of people every month, after his seminars. True, but he has his whole presentation on "Love" to win them over with first. And he wins them with his stories about his mama, his humor and his loving viewpoints on life. We are talking about the critical opening minutes of an interview. It takes time. Remember to step in slow.

As a speaker, I watch the body language of my audiences every day. The first minutes are tense and tight. Again, I'll see the arms folded or hands clasped in the lap or sometimes one foot half way out in the aisle. They are sizing me up and wondering if they are going to stay and listen or make a quick getaway. After the first hour, I'll see the arms stretched out across the back of the chair of the person next to them. The legs are crossed. The facial muscles are relaxed. The light is green and the body says, "I like it." Read the body message. The "natural" is ever so observant.

THE QUESTIONS: LIGHT AND BREEZY VS. HEAVY AND HARD!

Back to Barbara Walters again. When she interviews, her *timing* of questions and the *placement* of questions is superb. When she begins to interview, she wants to start with light and breezy questions that make the star or dignitary feel at home. She might say, "You played an entirely new role in your last picture, Paul. How did you prepare for it?" Nothing too personal, but she set the stage for a fair exchange of conversation between her and Newman. "Gee, your salad dressing is terrific. What got you started on that?" Light and breezy, fun, fun, fun!

Looking at you and me in the selling scene requires the same finesse. You must start the interview going by getting the customer to talk about something interesting to them. This comes about by asking questions that concern their family, lifestyle, hobbies and work. But don't try to evade the issue. Use an interview form when you first meet them and position the questions a certain way. They start out general and then go to specific. If some of you feel uncomfortable using a qualifying (but don't call it that) form for screening candidates for your product, let me share some thoughts on why you should change your mind regarding that viewpoint right now. First, the biggest heartaches in selling come from taking for granted certain details about your customers, for instance, their budget and financial situation or the need they have specifically in their lives for your product. You may spend countless hours with them going through benefits about your product. The conversation is mostly a demonstration of your competency and knowledge of the product but quess who's doing all the talking? You. The super naturals know that very little is said by the salesperson. They incite the buyer. They probe. They tickle. They provide stimulus to get the customer talking, opening up and confessing his or her need.

If this doesn't happen, you could end up with a whole bunch of unsold prospects. Prospects that you have "showed off" in front of. No one doubts that you are proficient in knowing the finer benefits of your product. But it's a one-way exchange. It reminds me of doing a one act one person show in a room with no windows and the door locked. It's a recitation. It's a robot talking to itself. The super naturals create energy, life and a flow back and forth between themselves and the people they are with. It's exciting. Let's begin the process.

THE CUSTOMER INTERVIEW, INCLUDING QUESTIONS

Prepare a form that highlights some of the following areas in your field that will help you determine your customer's needs. When the customer arrives, introduce yourself, watching the eyes and the body. Now if someone has referred you to these people (a mutual friend), mention that party before you begin the interview process. It will help to break down defense barriers: "I've heard so much about you from _____(so and so). Then give them my **Double Responsibility Script:**

"I'm in trouble if I don't give you first class service. I'll have two people (or families) disappointed. You and _____(referral's name). It's a privilege to have people referring customers to me. It's the highest form of praise in my field. I promise I'll live up to the compliment."

Wow! They feel so important and love to see you on the pressure cooker. It also puts the pressure on them to remain loyal. Here is this honest, hard working natural trying to do the job. They are thinking, "We've got to let them try for us."

My dad, Joe Barrett, was a great marketing man. If an out-of-state customer was flying in to see the company he worked for, all sorts of things would happen to this customer because of Dad. The person would get off the plane in Chicago and be greeted by an airline representative and a golf cart. Then the person would be driven to the baggage claim. "Greetings, sir, Mr. Barrett and the Seeburg Company welcome you." If he brought his wife, flowers were handed to her. The client felt important. The red carpet treatment went out. **The Double Responsibility Script** gives that same kind of feeling. The salesperson is really saying, "You are important. People are watching out for you and I feel the pressure to do an outstanding job."

If there is no third party referring the customer, greet them like this:

"Thanks for giving me the time and opportunity to discuss your needs. My first responsibility is to determine your needs and see if we can even work together." This is a bit of a *take-away*, which is great. Why? Because when customers first come in, they are not sure about us and our product. What you just said voices that fear out loud. ("See if we can even work together.") They breathe a quiet sigh

of relief. They are thinking, "I'm not stuck with this jerk and his product. I can always say it's not what I had in mind." Now, this immediately causes them to relax. Then we say:

"In order to do a better job for you, may I have the privilege (the naturals love this word and so do their customers) *of asking you some pertinent questions that will help all of us decide if this product fits your particular needs?"* Zip-a-dee-do-dah! Don't you love this stuff? Keep reading you natural-to-be, you!!!

Light and Breezy Questions

- ♦ How many are in your family?
- ♦ What are some favorite hobbies?
- ♦ You sound like you are from the midwest. Whereabouts?
- ♦ How did you and your spouse meet? (This is a real favorite of mine. People love to talk about how they met and fell in love and they think it's great that you sit there and listen so intently. By the way, I am such a romanticist that the question always does intrigue me.)
- ♦ What's the best time of the day for me to call you? I hate to interrupt your activities (this shows them you are considerate plus you get to work with them without interruption).
- ♦ What do you and your wife do for a living?
- ♦ What's the most enjoyable part of your job?
- ♦ How long have you been searching for this product?
- ♦ What will you use this product for?
- ♦ When will you use this product most?
- ♦ Who in your organization will use this?
- ♦ Are you using a similar service now?
- ♦ Can you give me a rough idea of what you're budgeting for a product such as this?

Heavier and Harder Questions

- ♦ "If we are fortunate enough today to strike exactly the correct note between us on what you need, will you be in a position to proceed to make a decision regarding this product?"
- ♦ "How can I better explain to you questions you have about this product?"

Practice both types of questions (in front of a mirror) and then role play the questions with people. For instance, get reactions from different age groups. Role play with Grandmother, Mom, a friend, a young male, a middle-aged person, a single and a married. See how this goes over with each age group and take input from their comments. The most important thing should be that the questions are clear and easy to understand. And, of course, make people feel comfortable.

Also, sometimes we say things louder and other times we drop our voice tone down. Customers want the interview to be private and discreet. It's uncomfortable if others sitting nearby can hear. This is important to recognize. When we ask the questions in an intimate, soft way with the customer, it also makes them feel like they are the only people in the world that we have time for. They love that exclusive feeling.

The Golden Rule

Another important aspect of the interview is remembering that silence is golden. I have seen salespeople go on and on not realizing the people were already sold on the product. The next thing you know, in the course of this unnecessary conversation, the salesperson talks everyone out of the sale. Let's take clothing for instance. A lady comes in to a store and sees a fur jacket she loves. She trys it on. Based on all the interviewing and need determination, the salesperson is aware that this customer can afford it. But the salesperson refuses to close and ask for the order. "Oh that coat looks striking on you. It's just the right color and so smart, so chic. Some people think furs are a waste of money out here in California, unless you travel a lot, but can you imagine not owning one?" Bong! She just blew it. The lady starts thinking, "Yes, I wonder how much I will use this? Will my husband think it's a waste?" Lots of self-doubting questions arise because the salesperson did something she didn't have a right to do—give an opinion when no one asked for one. If the salesperson is of the opinion that some people think furs are a waste in California, *shut up about it.* No one cares. Most of the time this is nervous talk on

the part of the salesperson. This comes out because we find ourselves in a position of babbling for two reasons: (1) We hate
pregnant pauses and feel like talking will take the discomfort away.
(2) We are *avoiding* asking for the order. *Talking* is an *avoidance*
behavior when we are afraid to ask. When great enthusiasm is
generated by the customer, don't say too much but definitely
encourage them. They are having fun. Don't take the fun out of
it. Do you know some salespeople feel so guilty about spending
money on themselves in their own personal life that they transfer
it to their customers? "I'd love a coat just like it, if I could afford
one." I've actually heard a salesperson say that to a customer.
That really takes the fun out of buying the coat. The customer is
thinking, "Who is this waiting on me, my mother?"

Become comfortable with silence. Sit back and watch the customer bask in the coat. Then add, "It's so smart on you. It brings
out the natural glow of your skin color." Say honest and sincere
observations and sense when the timing is right and begin weaving
into closing questions. "The temperature is due to drop even further tonight. Can you picture yourself wearing this to the Notre
Dame game this weekend? We will handle the close in chapter
seven. But keep in mind—silence is our golden rule and babbling
is redirecting our and the customer's purpose.

Officer O'Malley Says the Customer Is Wrong!

Officer O'Malley is right because he's a police officer and he just
checked his radar and this guy was going 15 miles over the speed
limit. In this case, the customer is wrong and O'Malley is writing
up the order. But you and I aren't cops! The customers are never
wrong. If they are buying from you, don't argue. Let's take the
lady with the coat again. Say she is rambling on about this coat
saying, "I love chinchilla, I love chinchilla." You very nicely say,
"This is lamb." She continues on about how wrong you are. Do
not argue with her. Say this, "I might have misread the manufacturer's label. Let me check with my manager because I'd feel
terrible if you thought you were buying a chinchilla and it's a
lamb. Or I'd feel miserable if what I was telling you was wrong

because I didn't study my inventory enough before displaying it."
You know this is lamb because you are a super natural and the
product is indelibly marked on your brain. But don't come across
that way or you'll make the customer feel *wrong* and that ain't
right. Unless you want to join Officer O'Mally's force. They are
always looking for more good cops!

Don't Be Afraid to Confess, Mr. Buyer

During the course of the interview, salespeople often miss some
cues from their customers. They are asking all the right questions,
which is good. They know their product line well. Let's think
about the insurance salesperson for a moment. Maybe this particular insurance person is a broker and can handle several different brands of insurance. But due to a higher commission split
on one of the companies that he brokers for, he tends to push
that company more to this customer. This new customer has already used Land Life Insurance and is really not dissatisfied with
the insurance, but rather is dissatisfied with the Land Life agent
and decides to move on. But the new agent is losing the customer
because the customer doesn't want to change insurance companies. They just want a more expensive policy and a new agent.
They almost feel as if they will hurt this new salesperson's feelings
if they do get Land Life Insurance again. The salesperson says,
"Of course I can handle getting you a new Land Life policy but
have you looked into Beauty Life? Beauty Life is a few cents more
but listen to the advantages." The customer may listen and then
say, "We will get back to you." They almost feel obligated to buy
Beauty Life from this agent because the agent is so high on the
stuff. So rather than hurt the salesperson's feelings, they say, "We'll
get back to you." What they really intend to do is search for
another agent who will shut up and write the policy they want.

What do you do as a salesperson, if out of good conscience you
prefer selling Beauty Life because it's a better policy? You give
them my **True Confessions or Honesty Script.** Here goes:

"I know you want to stick to Land Life. But let me point out Beauty Life. However, if you still feel confident with Land Life, then I'll be happy to handle it for you."

Now the same thing happens if you are picking out several products to show a customer but you don't have them all available to show. Say this:

"These are the things I've selected for you to look at, but if what you want isn't here, I can get it for you quickly." Say things like: *"I can change my game plan at a minute's notice."* Or: *"I can jump on this today if we don't find what you want."*

This instills loyalty and won't allow the customer to think that these are the only products you have and like. Therefore if he doesn't say he likes them, it will hurt your feelings. Some customers are so nice that they will not say a word. They will even act as if they like your product. They will say, "We will get back to you." Then they'll go buy somewhere else because they didn't want to confront you or hurt your feelings. Remember, they are buying. You are not buying. Let them know that if you didn't hit on what they wanted today, you have more resources to tap. *"Hang in there with me, Mr. and Mrs. Customer."* Also, tell them to be honest with you:

"If what I've selected doesn't meet your needs, tell me. I can change my game plan at a moment's notice. I know the business." It instills loyalty and honesty on the customer's part.

Today's Customer Is Tomorrow's Newspaper

During the course of the interview, never make statements that show the sale is more important to you than the people. Perhaps you sell used or resale products and are the middle person between the seller and the buyer. Never give personal information out about the seller. "Let's make them a ridiculous offer. He just lost his job and will sell this baby grand, antique piano, dirt cheap." If the buyer says to you, "What do you think they'll take?" say, "I know they'll take what they are asking ($7,500 or whatever), but if you want to negotiate, I'll try for you." In my own career, I have had repeat business because buyers have said to me, "Because you didn't reveal personal and confidential information about the sellers of the product, we thought if we ever sell this thing, we'll call you. We trust you."

The Naturals Listen Up

Once while doing a seminar, I asked one of the super naturals in my audience, "What's your secret?" They replied, "I let the customer do all the talking." How beautiful. The natural can sit back and let the customer have the spotlight. No showing off. No "I'll show you how great I am." Just easy listening. This gives the customer the opportunity to shine, not you. You and I are the vehicle for the customers to get what they want. We determine customer needs. You can't do that by endless chattering. We ask the question and then listen. I've watched customers monopolize an entire conversation and even talk themselves right into the purchase then look to the salesperson and say, "You did it again, Joe. You are some kind of a salesman!" Joe hardly said a word.

People from Chicago Like People from Chicago

You'll notice one of the questions under light and breezy was: "You sound like you are from the midwest. . ." Have you ever heard of the word *affinity?* The dictionary calls it a *likingness.* You are drawn to something when you have an affinity for something or someone. There are degrees of affinity. Some people seem to have a natural affinity toward certain people, groups or locations. For instance, I am a midwesterner (Chicago) by birth. I lived there the first 19 years of my life. I think the people from the midwest have great personalities, wonderful accents and go to the best restaurants (Chicago cooking). Maybe I am a little biased. When I first started my selling career in California and I was interviewing and asking clients questions, one of the things I would listen for was the accent. It seems half of the west were midwestern transplants. I would be asking questions like, "How long have you lived in this area?" "What do you think of this product so far?" As I was chatting with them, I would pick up an accent and I would hear the Chicago "baack" sound. I would then say, "Gee, you sound like you are from the midwest. Where abouts?" They'd say, "Chicago." I'd say, "No kidding. I am from Chicago too." The "me too" is a great way to build rapport during the asking questions stage of getting to know one another. Ker-plop—down goes the defense barriers. Why? Because we have a natural affinity towards one another. We were born in the same area, affected by similar values and we seem to agree faster on things due to our viewpoint.

Notice on T.V. how commercials try to show you that their product is okay because certain groups, who have a natural affinity toward each other, use it. For example, baseball players. A lot of people identify with baseball players. They are regular, all-American guys. You see baseball players you know, like and identify with drinking a certain kind of beer. You say to yourself, "This beer must be good."

People are influenced like that. You are from Chicago. I am from Chicago. I am okay, you are okay. With this natural affinity going for us, it is easier to ask questions and receive answers to these questions. There are a lot of things we scan for in order to build affinity with people: places where we were born, accents, kids, clubs, sports, situations (divorcees hanging around with other divorcees), age (retirement areas such as Leisure World for retired folk), pregnant with pregnant. (Have you ever seen just one pregnant woman going down the street? Usually there are two.) There is a natural attraction towards some people more than others. Why not be aware of that in your selling endeavors.

People say opposites attract. My feeling is "Not for long!" Like attracts like. If you find yourself selling your stuff to people who sometimes sound like you, think like you and have the same sense of humor as you, don't fight it. Isn't selling more workable when we can say "Me too!" Now let's insert another thought. You will notice higher or lower degrees of attraction for others, depending upon you and their mood. Example: The new salesperson feels insecure, uncertain, and wishy washy. Who does he often attract? Uncertain and indecisive clients who "don't know what they want."

These clients start driving the new salesperson crazy. It causes a downward spiral of problems. New baby salesperson says, "I must be terrible. I can't get these people to buy anything." The more new baby salesperson talks to himself like that, the longer the indecisive customers hang around. After all, why should they have to make up their minds. This salesperson is available at all times for nuts to hang around with.

The attraction changes on the outside as the attraction changes on the inside. The salesperson by chance makes a sale. That's what happened to me. I made my first sale by accident (more on that in a later chapter). The new salesperson purposely doesn't want to recognize the time to close. Why? Because they fear acceptance. People talk about fearing rejection, but let me tell you, we also fear acceptance. We help people buy something and then we worry. "What if they don't like it. They will blame me."

Back to the attraction idea. We make the sale and guess what? Self-confidence goes up. Self-esteem rises. Soon more confident buyers float in. Why? Because we are more confident. We got some good self-talk going. We are saying things like, "I must be pretty good. I did a good job. Bring on the customers."

It only makes sense that we attract what we feel and then pull that type of response in. I swear that is how I found my husband. A while after my first marriage broke up, I threw myself in work and felt, "Well, at least, I can do this well." But as time went on, even though I wasn't hooked up to anyone, I gave myself credit for being a pretty good mom and worker. That's when my old friend, Mike, came into the picture. He likes happy people. He hates complainers. He hates moaners. We began dating and both of us were finally feeling pretty good about ourselves as individuals and we decided we had a winning combination.

Once the basic affinity is built in, is that enough? No. A question was posed to Barbara Walters once about how she managed to finally get interviews that others couldn't seem to get. She said she just never gave up nicely bugging them. Dropping little notes, quick phone calls and lots of pleasantries. In other words—following through. Have you ever known salespeople who conduct tons of interviews? Everybody is their friend, but that's as far as it goes? Usually that's because they get the fire going but can't or don't want to keep it ignited. It takes not only affinity, but the tenacity to hang in there until it is going to fly.

THE JOB INTERVIEW:
THE INTERVIEW THAT SELLS YOU

Most of this chapter has been dedicated to the customer interview to determine that particular customer's product needs. But what about another important interview—the job interview. We are now the one being interviewed. What are we buying? A job or maybe even a career. It's an audition. How we answer the questions and how we pose questions back to the interviewer will determine if we win and achieve our goal. The naturals always interview to win and get the job they target for.

Where Do I Begin?

Are you just joining or coming back into the job market? Conduct informational interviews everywhere you go. Do this at cocktail parties, while chatting with friends, at the gas station, bank or airport. Just ask people what they do and how they do it. Students who are almost out of high school or college should ask a million questions to teachers, family, friends or total strangers that do things in their field of interest. Prospect your career. It's good practice for real interviews. "I'm looking into future possibilities. Tell me about your job. What activities are you responsible for each day? What do you like least and best?"

It's good to find out exactly what people do because often a job seems glamourous. Take an airline steward or stewardess. It involves a lot of tasks you would do in the kitchen or at a restaurant job. But the travel and chance of serving many different folks may more than compensate. It depends on you. The idea is to break down different businesses. Ask the individuals you talk to if you can mention their name (especially if they know you or your family and think well of you) at the time of that specific job interview. When you are prospecting careers and asking individuals questions, ask them if there are other people in that field you can talk to. Often, someone who is a real expert in the field would be willing to have a brief chat with you over the phone. Many times, people who want to be speakers will call me up and ask me questions. The National Speaker's Association has a mentor–student program, which allows new people to ask pros how it's done and what it takes to build a career in my field. I always refer them on to National Speakers Association.

Don't Believe the Sizzle

Often, classified ads make a job sound like heaven on earth. The purpose of the ad is to get the phones to ring, just like selling any other product. Don't assume a thing. Before you make an appointment, ask them questions too. Ask what the job entails. "I see in your ad you are looking for a marketing representative. Does this involve travel and approximately how much?"

The 15-Minute Critique

A few months ago, I was looking for a maintenance company or person to clean our home once or twice a week. I got a postcard in the mail around the same time I had the need. It was a caricature of Carol Burnett and her mop. (Remember when she use to do the cleaning lady routine? Her show opened with the cartoon on the screen.) The card said: "Call Carol for cleaning." I thought: "How clever!" I called Carol and she sounded *pretty* enthusiastic. I set up an interview with her. She broke one appointment and was late for the other. Also, she pulled up in a van that looked like it needed about three weeks of hard-core cleaning. Bad image for a cleaning lady. After speaking to her for a few moments, I got the impression she'd come when she wanted to and not when

I needed her. I could have been dead wrong, but first impressions count to the person passing out the change.

Some Don'ts

Some *don'ts* for the interview are: Don't smoke, don't drink (if it's a lunch interview or if you are in an executive office with a bar) and don't ask dumb questions. I knew a young college grad who got so nervous during a pregnant pause during a job interview that she threw this in: "How long do we get for lunch?" We've got a real worker on our hands here! Also, don't mention personal problems. "I have to pick my child up from the baby sitter at 5:15 P.M. Will working late ever be required?" No one is interested in your personal problems. We've all got them and the thing to do is handle them and shut up.

Use Pre-Approach Information

Prior to the interview, you should have talked to people in the field. You researched the company and conducted your own methods of investigation. Use that knowledge for your benefit now. "I understand 80 percent of the widget market was captured by your division last year. Your advertising was everywhere. What other means worked? It must make you proud." Show interest and intelligence and remember: Flattery will get you everywhere. The more you can *naturally* (not artificially) compliment the person who is interviewing you, the better. However, it must be based on fact. "Your reputation out in the field, in the area of packaging, is truly envied. How many years of experience do you think it takes? Did you have any mentors?"

Know the "This Is Your Life" Question

Almost every job interview with a future contains this question: "Where do you want to be in five years?" Prepare for it prior to the interview. If you act dumbfounded it could cost you the job.

What's the Money Honey?

Don't bring up salary. Let them. If asked specifically and it's in a line of work you are proficient at, try this: "My previous income has been _____. I was hoping to get in the _____ range, if given the opportunity of obtaining this position."

Boy Am I Smart

There is nothing worse than acting as if you know an answer when you don't. The employer says, "Are you familiar with the X1O computer in your present position?" You retort, "Oh yes, I program it daily into my SpeedyType typewriter." The person gives you a strange look and says, "They don't have a SpeedyType hook-up." You sit there, wanting to put the head between the knees and hide. Just be honest. Be yourself. That's all people want.

Look How Chic I Am

Clothing is important, but make it simple. Too much jingle and jangle draws attention to the *things* on you, not you. Whenever I see a male or female decked out from stem to stern in gold, I get preoccupied. Clothing should be smart and simple. Crisp shirts and blouses, nicely tailored suits and just plain "Dial soap" and clean all over is nice. A slight scent of aftershave or cologne only completes the picture. Too much makes one want to get sick and often interrupts the interview for a bathroom visit.

Keep Those Questions Coming!

Be sure to ask a lot of questions. "What can the person you hire do to make your department efficient?" Don't say "What can I do?" I never like to assume it's going to be me. A little humility goes a long way. "Will the person selected have the privilege of visiting the representatives in the field much?" While you ask questions, common denominators will come up. Guess who's son is on the same soccer team? Guess who's wife plays a lot of tennis? Same principle applies with selling yourself on the job that we use with the customer and the product. Likes attract likes. People enjoy hiring people who have similar viewpoints and values. Rebels aren't looked upon too keenly. Another winning question is "Tell me about the person who previously held the position. Why did they leave?" This allows you, the applicant, to protect yourself. It gives you some insight into how they have treated past employees. If you find out for instance, that the person holding the job previously was promoted—terrific. That means good work will be recognized and there is a chance for promotion within the department down the road. You must also be aware that they may ask you a similar question. "Why are you leaving your company?" Be prepared to answer that one.

Tie Down with a Time Planner

My time planner has notepaper in it. I hope yours does. It is important to take notes during the interview. It shows you are interested and helps you remember important future tips to carry out. Tie down the person with this: "Which would be more convenient? Shall I call back today or tomorrow to see what has transpired?" Then use your appointment calendar to slot in the time, date and place. It shows you are with it! Spring-loaded and ready to go.

I Brought Some Good Stuff

Bring out the testimonial letters and letters of recommendation, if you have any. Be sure you wait until you are near the end of the interview. These are critical and remain in people's minds. Try this approach. "I feel it's important for you to get a little history about me and my track record. So, I do have a short portfolio of testimonial letters." The portfolio may be a small album that fits into your briefcase or purse. Make sure you can easily get to it. All they have to do is open it and some of the heavyweights who love you will stand out.

What About a Résumé?

Be careful. Some of them are too slick. If the job is in the field of advertising and they look at stuff like that great. People interviewing don't want to feel you are on automatic. Thousands of these things have been pumped all over America. It takes away the personal touch and credibility. Every company wants to feel you really just want to work for them.

Interlock All Past Experience

Last summer, my daughter Beth was applying for several jobs for vacation. Her previous experience during Christmas and Easter was selling in a dress shop. She was hoping to get a job as a waitress or hostess in a restaurant. When she was selling clothes, she won the monthly award for most sales. Beth was good at working with the public and obviously had people skills. People skills are required in restaurants too. When they asked her at the restaurant if she had previous restaurant experience as a hostess, she said, "No," and dropped it. I told her all previous jobs can prepare us for the present situation. A better way to have handled that question might have been "Well, restaurant work means a lot of people contact and I've had plenty of that. In my previous job, I won the top award for serving customers who came to our shop. I know I would represent your restaurant with those same skills." Dynamite. And they love the quick, sharp response. It shows you are on the ball. Just because you didn't specifically sell widgets in your last job doesn't necessarily disqualify you. Look for the skill that would be common to both past and present position and emphasize it with this employer.

Keep Those Cards and Letters Coming

Immediately following the interview, go directly to a mailbox and send a thank you note. Or deliver it to the secretary the following day.

> I appreciate the opportunity you gave me to discuss career possibilities with you. If selected, I would give 100 percent of my capabilities and consider it a privilege to be on *your team*. Thanks for talking with me.

People do not follow up enough. Never take anything for granted. Never *expect* in life. Only give and watch what comes back. You won't be able to keep up with the jobs, opportunities, challenges, people, places and events that come crashing your way. It's exhausting and it's ever so naturale!

CHAPTER **5**

THE NATURAL GLOW OF A GOOD PRESENTATION

Set the Stage ◆ *Try the Take-Away—*
Today ◆ *Danny's Directives to Demonstrate By . . .*
Take a Deep Breath; Stop Signs; Customer's Involvement;
Things Gone Unnoticed; Don't Oversell; Patience, Please;
Afford Me; Special Details; Stuck in the Middle; Beware
of the Good Guys; Check the Tone; The First Time Is the
Best Time

K assie Fehnske owns one of the finest exercise studios in the country, "The Exercise Express." Imagine you were greeted at the door of her studio by a depressed and unenthusiastic aging woman saying: "Join us for some fitness." How would you react? Wouldn't you feel the overall credibility of the studio was lacking? Instead, let me describe the "real" Kassie. At thirty eight years of age Kassie has the body, energy, and enthusiasm of a sixteen-year-old girl. Kassie, the mother of four children, conducts one of the most advanced aerobic and stretch classes I have encountered any-where. Her presentation is filled with exciting music, moves and motivation. Her outfits are striking and pleasing to look at. Her energy is the same for each class, sometimes, that is, after four previous one-hour workouts. You would never know the differ-ence. If there are five in the class or fifteen, she gives. Her pre-sentation has that natural glow.

Why describe Kassie in a sales book? Because she is selling. She is selling her studio and her classes. The other instructors she hires all reflect her dedication. Two of her original teachers that started with Kassie come to my mind this moment. Their names are Patti and Roberta. Patti Robinson is a strong vivacious women in her twenties who just amazes me. Her energy and charisma with her classes motivate every one of us who work with her. Her laugh and style just delight all. I love to be a part of her class. Roberta Riddle has a dance background, just as Kassie and Patti do, but she also has the unique ability to choreograph so many interesting aerobic numbers. She is beautiful and graceful and does her classes with such ease that she gives me motivation in a entirely different way than Patti. Both are excellent instructors and presenters of their art form.

It might be interesting to note that one of her instructors is a bit overweight. But she has a terrific personality, is a great dancer and very light on her feet. Her appearance is impeccable and having her as an instructor carries an interesting message. "I am qualified to teach even though I am overweight. I am not embarrassed to help myself and others." She teaches beginning classes and it really is an inspiration for the women who come to the first couple of classes overweight and self-conscious. They feel as if there is hope. You will hear me mention "purity of intention" in this book. That is the clear-cut intention of people who have a deep desire to do the greatest good for their customer, their student or whoever they are involved with. That is what shines through all the instructors eyes at the "Exercise Express."

It really doesn't matter what your lot in life happens to be. Whatever you present, present it with flair. That's what the naturals do. I cannot help but think about an airline flight I was on last week. The airline steward really had a class act. Talk about turning a very ordinary job into something special. Most of us riding on an airplane hardly notice the early directions for use of the oxygen mask or seat belt that the airline people demonstrate. This particular night, everyone was typically half asleep or reading a good magazine. I was with my daughter Mary on the flight and we both had our eyes half closed. We must have felt some strange energy or vibration in the air. For some reason, we looked up and saw this young male steward doing a very ordinary thing in an extraordinary way. Suddenly, he had the flare of a magician as he whipped the oxygen mask first to the left, then to the right. Then with a quick snap, he pulled the band behind the mask that goes over the head. Then with another hand he whisked the seat belt in the air and showed us how to snap it on and off. He had the moves of the mime, Marcel Marceau. Mary and I looked around and watched him take a half-asleep airplane and turn it around to a bunch of bright eyes and bushy tails. His presentation glowed. And yet every day, across lots of friendly skies, hundreds of airline people are preoccupied watching another steward or stewardess go through the boring part of their job.

SET THE STAGE

First and foremost, a perfect setting helps before conducting our presentation. Our airline steward knew exactly where everything was so that sight unseen, a fingertip could grasp what he needed to do his demonstration. If you are marketing big ticket items such as cars, houses, furniture and jewelry, it is important to remember to ask yourself the following questions: How's the lighting? Am I displaying something in a showroom? Is the place neat and picked up? For instance, I worked in a model home complex in the late sixties for a large builder. Often, the crew that was on duty before me left old coffee cups, papers and cigarette butts in ashtrays. It was my responsibility to run around, empty trash, turn on lights plus soft music and give quick dust checks before the public arrived.

As a clothing salesperson in college, I needed to get the proper lighting on the mannequins, check to be sure their outfits weren't handled and looking less than crisp and give the department one quick touchup before showtime. Also, I checked the racks of clothes to see if they were back on the hangers correctly and organized by size. Did I have my cash register ready to go and the sales slips handy? Was I on my toes?

This all sounds so basic and simple. But do you realize how many people are not in the present moment when they begin their day? The curtain goes up and they miss the opportunity to do what they can to make the most of each presentation. It is the little simple stage preparations that tend to make the performance glow. If you sell anything from computers to cosmetics be sure the product doesn't look man handled from the day before. Put the product into the present just as you do to yourself. Is there a special sale in the newspaper you should be aware of? Often, salespeople are at a loss for words because they didn't check what's new for today.

Recently, we purchased a five-pound typewriter for airplane use (which I have since returned). The salesperson had no idea how to work it and there it was out on display for him to demonstrate. Again because Michael and I are an easy sell, we took it home to "figure it out." It is so frustrating being handled that way.

What about you? Maybe you are the product and the demonstration is you sitting at a reception desk. Perhaps you greet the public at a bank or a corporate headquarters. Do you look fresh and cheery? Is your desk clear and unencumbered? Are you ready to greet the public with a smile? The receptionist, hostess, secretary, mail clerk and grocery clerk all set the stage and the mood with their appearance and their smiles. What is your message? "Get out of here, you are interrupting my day." Or "Come on in, you are making my day!" My grampa Daniel used to say, "Smile and the world smiles with you, weep and you weep alone. For the cheerful grin will get you in where the kicker is never known."

The telephone glow is an important part of your presentation too. Many sales trainers recommend placing a mirror in front of your face while on the phone. Not a dumb idea. The words are meaningless without the glow and warmth that comes from a happy telephone voice. All over the country, operators, phone canvassers, etc. decide their fate with a smile and a word transmitted to a receiver. Does your phone voice say "come hither" or "go yonder?"

Other little things must be noted as part of setting the stage. Odors? What does the setting smell like? Get rid of bad odors with a fresh air spray. Trying to sell a product in a stale environment distracts. Also, if there are sweet odors such as food, use the smell to entice. One time a department store had a special on "woks." Lo and behold they had an in-house cook preparing the oriental favorite in the middle of the kitchen section of the store. Giving out free samples merely added to the chance of making the wok sales. Whether or not some of us had ever considered using a wok or not, we were all walking out with woks. (Hey I like that—walk with a wok.)

I cannot think of a better setting of perfect staging for a sale than my friend Mary Rubenstein's clothing boutique called "Mi Place" in Laguna Niguel, California. On one side of her shop you find yourself entering into a fast paced nail salon called "Accent on Nails" owned by Teri Duckworth. Get your nails done and while you are waiting for your piggy toes and fingers to dry, buy a dress or two. Enter the other side of the shop and slip through a door and you will be in the company of some of the greatest hair designers in the south county of southern California—"Wall Street Hair Design." "Wall Sreet" is owned by Bill Wall and Marilyn Maxick. My favorite hairdresser, Larry West, abides there too. If you get stuck waiting for your busy hairdresser, you can browse through the famous "Mi Place" for a new sweater or a pair of shoes. All three owners (nail shop, hair design and clothing boutique) have gotten together and created about as much synergy as you could imagine. When the ladies get their hair done, one of the hair stylists might ask, "Are you all ready for New Year's Eve? You should see what Mary has just gotten into the store. Only one lady will show up in the outfit at this party." The next thing you know, you find yourself just taking a quick peek at whatever Mary just got in hot off the racks. Maybe you are getting your nails done and you notice that one of the manicurists is wearing a new "Mi Place" frock. All three owners use each other's products. The nice nails, hair styles or fashions can be seen on any of the owners or the people that work for them so they are in essence selling every moment.

The clientele are mostly career women who have their own money to spend or the wives of professional men who have plenty of spending money. She caters to people who wear expensive designer clothes. She imports the best labels from New York and you just won't see her fashions in the ordinary department store. Rarely will you see a woman walk out of the nail or hair salon without a new dress, sweater or pair of slacks. Here you are in this relaxed state pampering yourslf and in comes Mary to tantalize you with some gorgeous new fashions. The key here has been to set the stage for the mood of the customer. Most women getting their hair and nails done are in a pampered mood. Why not pamper yourself even further with a new suit or dress? With Mary there, knowing her product so well and exactly what will look good on you, the whole scene becomes a natural.

TRY THE TAKE-AWAY—TODAY

One thing that Mary Rubenstein does that I like is treat her product with respect. Her attitude is this: "This suit is not for everyone who sees it, the discriminating woman—but not every woman." When we have respect for our product, we handle it like it is gold and we create a mystique around the product. This also gives the impression that my product is special and if you are lucky I will let you purchase it.

Now keep in mind we do not do this to manipulate or be snobby. It's just that we have so much affinity for what we sell that it is important to us that our product get into the right hands and is appreciated. How do I teach you this? I can't. The only thing I can tell you is the more educated you are about the product that you market, the easier it will be for you to use the **Take-Away Script** that I briefly mentioned in chapter four. Here is the **Take-Away Script:**

"If we find, after interviewing you and researching your needs, that this product can compliment your lifestyle—terrific. But it has to be right."

Many times I have taken home a dress that I saw in Mary's shop and she has said, "I don't think that is you." She knows what I like that well. Sure enough I take it home and I am lost in a dress that I don't like. The take-away idea is based on ethics, not manipulation. When you know what you are doing you will not market a product to everyone and anyone just to make a buck.

DANNY'S DIRECTIVES TO DEMONSTATE BY . . .

Let's assume that the stage is ready to go and you are about as well versed as possible concerning the product and the customer.

You have done your homework with the prospect and the interview, according to the tips given to you in chapter four. We are
about to demonstrate our wares and we must be sure that all goes
well. Try these dozen thoughts and interject them into your presentation and see if it doesn't fine tune it the way you want it.

1. *Take a deep breath, take your time and love the product.* When
I was a new baby in sales, I rushed through everything because
I was a nervous wreck. I didn't realize how fast I was rushing
through my presentations just to get them over with. After all, I
felt I didn't know what I was talking about so the sooner I could
get through this the better off I would be. Also, I would then know
the outcome. Would they buy or wouldn't they buy? God knows
they probably won't so if I hurry I can get to the bad news fast.
Crazy, but that is how our mind works, when we are skulking
through new territory. So, just get into the present moment. Touch
a wall. The desk. Take a stretch. Handle your product, if it is
something you can handle. Start out slow. Use pauses and again
show lots of affinity for your product. (Afffinity means a fondness
or likingness.)

I can remember my friend, Patrick McVay, giving me a great tip
after I wrote my first sales book. I was so proud of it. But during
a seminar I felt very uncomfortable trying to sell or push this book
down my audience's throat. I had become the natural salesperson
behind closed doors. And that was it. I couldn't imagine selling
in front of five hundred people into a microphone. McVay said
to me, "Do you love your book?" I said, "Of course I do." After
four years of love and hard work being mustered into that book,
the reaction was strong. He then instructed me to hold the book,
feel the book, turn the pages and contemplate the hours, weeks,
months and years of preparation and experience with the public
(both sad and joyful) that went into the creation of that book. He
told me to walk around with it a lot in my room, flying on an
airplane or just at home. I started doing it and making that book
part of myself. God knows it is an extension of myself, my hopes,
my beliefs and how to's for salespeople in the real estate field.
Then he suggested I carry the book with me on stage, refer to it
and use certain quotes or passages from it at differents points

during the presentation. Eventually, I did all this and came to a point in my program where I formally presented the book to the audience with so much love, admiration and affinity for my product that it was a "natural" request for me to want that audience to buy and have that book. Today, the book ranks tops in the real estate textbook field for agents. I noticed on T.V. not so long ago that Dr. Robert Schuller, on his Sunday morning T.V. show, held his book *Tough Times Never Last; Tough People Do* the whole time he was speaking.

So, you love your product to death. As you begin your presentation, speak slowly and ask the customer to interrupt you if there is anything that they do not understand. To overcome your early nervousness, you may want to say to the customer:

"Sometimes I get so involved, I go too fast or miss a customer's quizzical look about a point of concern or interest. Please stop me if I do that."

Also, ask them to be honest with you and speak frankly about things in the demonstration that they do or don't like. *"It won't hurt my feelings if there are certain qualms you have."* Make the presentation go smoothly by making it okay for you and the customer to express honest feelings throughout the entire encounter together. This of course requires you to know even more about your product but I am assuming that is the only way you would have it anyway.

2. *Signs of misunderstanding should be stop signs.* When you see a customer yawn, stare or use body language that denotes boredom, stop. You can be sure that you took the customer past his point of understanding. Maybe it was a word that you used. The example that I continually think about is a computer. Recently, I purchased a personal computer. Many times, during the presentation, I found myself yawning or letting my thoughts drift into the past or future. I was lost because something had been said that I pretended I understood but didn't. The rest of the presentation was downhill for me. Please be so aware of the customer that you can continually know that he is following your train of thought. As a public speaker, I have gotten to the point where, if in a room of one thousand people, one person is lost, I can spot it. I then stop and look at that person and repeat the word or the point I made. People are ever so grateful when you do that. No

one likes to admit they are lost, but when we have the sensitivity to see it, we not only have made a friend but possibly saved a sale.

3. *Use customer involvement.* Does your product or service allow for customer involvement during the presentation? Cosmetics, computers, cars, even houses, create a great deal of customer involvement during the presentation. When I sold homes, often I would have the customers sit alone in the living room and picture their furniture in it when we returned for the second time. The car salesperson allows the customer a test drive. The cosmetic ladies give a free facial with lots of involvement from the customer. In computers, customers are having a ball putting a program together for home shopping or home accounting. How exciting to hit a computer menu that spits outs information about the weather in Hawaii or the great plays available to see in New York. You might do about one third of your presentation (enough to give the customer understanding and curiosity about the product) and then begin to create the customer involvement. Try saying this:

"At this point I want to give you the opportunity to get a feel for what our paper planes are all about. Would you like to try manuveuring one just for fun?"

The words "just for fun" take the edge off the step into involvement required to make a closing decision.

4. *Point things out they haven't noticed.* Recently, a friend of mine began using a specialized method of skin care. She went on a trial period of one month with the product and noticed a lot of her blemishes beginning to clear up, using their makeup base. After one month, she went back for a follow-up check and the woman gave her some interesting information about the doctor who discovered the product. She mentioned that he was a dermatologist and he created some wonderful things in his laboratory that only certain lucky women had the opportunity to experiment with on their skin. A lot of famous women had skin problems and heard about the doctor's methods and began going to him for treatment. Just as other good news always travels fast, so did his story and soon he was asked to market his product. My friend never knew the product was created by a doctor or even that certain medicinal solutions were in his makeup base. She herself got caught up in

the story. The more the saleslady talked about the uniqueness of that product, the more my friend wanted it for herself.

During your presentation you might want to say something like:

"This typewriter is different from other standards. With an adapter, it can be hooked up to your personal computer."

Do not take things for granted. Do not assume that the customer knows this typewriter has an adapter. Things that *are not* obvious should be pointed out. Things that *are* obvious should not be pointed out. In real estate, we use to tell the new ones: "Don't say—this is the kitchen." Tee hee you dummy, I bet you thought it was a bathroom!

5. *Do not oversell or push too hard.* Have you ever worked with a salesperson that pushed entirely too hard? It almost made you wonder if the item you were thinking of buying was "hot." The salesperson was ramming it down your throat. Always be respectful of buyers and understand that the decision to buy ultimately is in their hands. Some will tell you that once you corner customers, do not let go until they buy. I never found that philosophy too appealing. For one thing I can always return the item as soon as the pushy salesperson leaves my life. Usually if a product or service is everything it should be, and the salesperson is everything he or she should be, the sale will be consummated.

6. *Be patient.* The bigger the item, the longer the decision time, particularly when you are dealing with conservative people. Let's say, for instance, your product involves comparision shopping. Other brands, warranties, etc, come into play. Let the buyers know you are patient and that you are confident in your product to stand the test of time. I would rather have them comparision shop before the purchase than after. Why? It's too heartbreaking thinking you made the deal click and then later to find out it was a premature close.

7. *Use affordability in your presentation.* Sometimes we think that people have no attention units on money because they appear so affluent. I have found that the more affluent people are, the more watchful they become of the dollar. People with money know that the word is out about them. "They've got the bucks." Consequently, they think that folks want to rip them off because their attitude is a few dollars down the drain won't bother Mr. and

Mrs. Got the Bucks. Wrongo. One of the ways they were able to make their money was to know value and know where it was going. So don't be afraid to say: "The beauty about this product is it's affordability ranks lower than it's true value."

8. *Be careful about details.* When you demonstrate, keep in mind that if you haven't pointed out every detail obvious or not regarding your product, it will be a whole lot easier to get your customer's attention when you do open your mouth to speak. If you have not allowed certain facts to sink in, using the pregnant pause, then a lot of the silly details you are pointing out will go in one ear and out the other. You know the naturals by the way they can command attention. When they open their mouth the customers know it is going to be something good. You haven't rambled on about the top of the cold cream jar or the steering wheel of the car for the first half hour with the result of totally losing them. You know the majors from the minors. Too much detail talk can be exhausting to a buyer.

9. *Do not get in the middle.* Are you working with two parties that are purchasing together? Are they disagreeing? Don't ever take sides in your presentation. What happens if it is obvious that one party is flowing with you and the other isn't? Stop. The worse possible thing you can do is side with one of them. Possibly the one that you think holds the purse strings is the party with the least power. Recently, Cher was interviewed in *Cosmopolitan* magazine and gave a surprising revelation that happens in lots of households. She mentioned that even though she looked like the dominant one on the "Sonny and Cher Comedy Hour" 10 years ago, it was strictly an act. Her little digs to Sonny made it sound that way. At home he had the say on decisions. Keep that in mind in *all* presentations. Take this position: "There is nothing worse for me than to market my product to a couple that do not agree. The first thing we must do is talk about the points in disagreement. Try listing all things that you are liking and disliking. If you need time to be alone together, please tell me. I can excuse myself or perhaps we can resume our appointment another day. I want you both to be happy."

10. *Be careful of the good guys.* Have you ever done a presentation with individuals and they loved everything about your product?

You probably kept saying to yourself, "This is too good to be true." Right. It probably is. People who do not object to anything, sometimes, can't afford what you are showing them. Or they could be the type that want everyone, including you the salesperson, to love them. They cannot possibly bring themselves to tell you what they like or do not like about an item or service. You need to be a bit more forward and blunt with people like this. "It is really important that we open up the lines of communication between us. I need to know exactly what is affordable to you and whether or not you love this product as you seem to indicate. I do not want to waste your time or mine. Do not be worried about hurting my feelings." I have seen too many salespeople go on for days with people who are basically bored and need entertainment.

11. *Follow the customer's emotional tone.* I have found that it is better for the salesperson to blend into the mood of the buyers during the onset of presentation than to come off too excited and enthusiastic before they are ready. If you sense that the buyers are not looking forward to this presentation, but this is a product that they need, cool it a bit. As they see your competence and natural affinity toward the product, their enthusiasm will build and soon you can bring them up based on your expertise. However, there is nothing worse than coming on too strong and finding that the people are being distracted by your phony enthusiasm. I just think people enjoy working with a human being, not a superficial robot.

12. *Act as if everytime is your first time.* Yul Brynner recently performed in *The King and I* for the 4,000th time. People seeing him thirty years after his first performance as the infamous King of Siam report he has the energy, drive and motivation that he displayed thirty years ago. And here's another interesting addition to this incredible man. In 1983, while he was performing in Los Angeles in *The King and I*, it was reported he was going through chemotherapy treatments for cancer. Now there's a true super, super, super, natural. And for most of those performances in 1983, no one knew he was sick. On top of all of this, we have to call Yul Brynner a great salesperson. He has sold the audience on the King and *The King and I*.

Everytime you begin your presentation and go all the way

through the entire shooting match, people should get the feeling that you are doing it for them just like you had never done it before. This looks a lot easier than it actually is. That means you click off all personal problems, other professional problems and distractions and simply go for the moment with true verve.

Imagine Yul Brynner receiving cancer therapy in the morning and doing *the King and I* to a capacity audience each night. Not quite as dramatic, imagine Jimmy Connors winning the 1983 U.S. Open Tennis Tournament with a bad case of diarrhea and a very sore toe. He was allowed one break in the middle of the match to handle his problems. He won that match beating someone years younger than he. He won that game mentally, certainly not physically. He was in no mood to play tennis that day and his body was giving him the worst possible signals it could muster up. But his presentation on national T.V. and on that court that day, was graceful, natural and tough. We can learn so much from these examples. Learning to control our thoughts and keeping our intention right on the customer helps tremendously. For Yul Brynner, the customer to be pleased is the audience. We are all performing. Only some do it the super natural way.

CHAPTER **6**

A NATURAL REACTION:
"I OBJECT, MAYBE?"

Eight Natural Reactions People Experience When They
Decide to Buy ◆ *Six Ways to Remove the Sting From*
Any and All Objections

The question we must really ask ourselves, when we hear customers object, is this: "Are they objecting or just talking to themselves out loud?" Remember that customers are about to make a closing decision. When buyers make a closing decision, they naturally react in fear, which causes an objection to appear. The larger the ticket items, the louder the nerves and the mouth rattle. Do not go trying to handle a objection when it may only be a little self-talk. There is a difference you know! People only object infrequently in the close. What they are actually doing is making a lot of comments or basically talking to themselves. Do you talk to yourself when you are getting ready to buy something? I do.

Last year our family moved. We had lived in the same house for 12 years. Although we were all ready for the change, it tended to panic me. They say on a list of ten stresses in life, moving is high on top of the list. I began noting some of the things that I did during this changing time in my life. Here I had worked with people for ten years in real estate and realized I had begun taking for granted the enormous decision that is required for people to move. Actually, this applies to all people buying anything. But because the home is such a big ticket item, imagine that all the feelings and reactions are amplified. I felt like a walking contradiction as I tried to decide whether I wanted to buy or not. I had both buyer's bliss and remorse. I was telling myself I was thrilled to death to have this chance to grab this wonderful new way of life and, on the other hand, I wondered, "Can we handle this?"

At that point, the whole family started self-talking. First, I started calculating the new payment and how much more money it would be. Then the kids started muttering something about schools. Would they be able to go to the same school? Kevin, my son the gymnast, started wondering if he had to give up gymnastics. Then my husband started moaning about how we had the house we were living in all fixed up exactly the way we wanted it and we would have to start from scratch again.

Then the talk started going the other way. Here we had the chance to move two blocks from the beach. My son Daniel is a great surfer. Now he could surf every day after school. Then we started talking about the extra space we would finally have. And wouldn't it be great not to have to do the laundry in the garage anymore. This house had an indoor place for laundry. The talk just kept rambling on continuously. If a salesperson had been present, I hoped they would remember an important point: "Shut up and ignore these nervous people for the moment."

People go through a true metamorphosis at the time they make a decision to do something different. They argue with themselves and almost carry on a debate about what they should do. Don't we do that in the store, when trying to decide if we should buy that expensive suit or not? "Gosh, I really love it, but how am I going to pay for it? I won't get a Visa bill for another 45 days. After all, my girlfriend's wedding is coming up and I cannot be seen in that same old messy outfit. And remember no Visa payments for 45 days, so you might say for today, I am actually getting the whole outfit free." Don't we go on and on?

Now what if a salesperson pops in with a retort to one of our comments? Maybe I am saying something like this, "Well I really like it, but I was hoping to get a pink suit this time." Salesperson comes back with this remark: "Oh I bet pink wouldn't look as good on you as this blue outfit does." Then the customer starts thinking, "What the heck is this guy talking about? I have a whole room full of pink stuff and now this creep tells me pink isn't my color. I guess I look lousy in everything. Forget this." The customer walks out of the store in a tiff. See how saying something at the wrong time can make customers mad and cause them to forget the flow of self-talk that was happening in their mind?

The point that salespeople forget is if the customer is self-talking, then they are definitely getting ready to make a decision. Nobody talks to themselves unless they are excited. You should have seen these friends of mine when they bought their first boat. They went on and on. "Did you see the fly bridge? Did you check out the fighter chairs, but oh heck, it's not a wood boat and that is what I really wanted. Doggone it, I knew there was something about this goofy boat I didn't like. Oh look here did you notice this fabulous area below where you can cook and sleep?" Different people have different ways of self-talking. The quiet ones do this in their heads and the extroverts do it out loud. Either way, don't sweat it. The salesperson should be excited because you are close to pay dirt here. Remember how it was to go fishing and that crazy fish would start nibbling the worm. Then he would think, "Hey, is this for real or phony," and he begins to back off. But if it tasted real good, he'd come back for more. Especially if he is hungry. And of course, if the need is there, you'd have caught the fish.

There is one major point I want to make about objections. Some buyers cannot come to a decision to purchase, even if they need it or can afford it. Why? Because of self-esteem and feelings of guilt. I knew someone who actually came close to buying a brand new Cadillac but backed out because mentally he hadn't caught up to his new financial status. I have heard celebrities comment that after they had banked their 11th million, they still find themselves wondering if they should splurge and buy something that they always wanted. This happens because we think we do not deserve to have what we now have. There is nothing a salesperson can do in extreme cases like this. These people probably need counseling regarding their new lifestyle. They need lessons on how to enjoy what they have earned without fear. Often, they are afraid they'll go off the deep end and in a fit of spending blow everything they have worked hard for up to this point.

In normal cases, if it is right for buyers to purchase your product, then trust them to buy it. I always have said that handling objections shouldn't be a major issue, if you did your homework.

This means the salesperson should be totally familiar with what goes on in every department of his company. If you sell computers, even though you are not an engineer or a technician type, have you totally familiarized yourself with all aspects of the computer?

My husband and I own Danielle Kennedy Productions. Most people think that this is strictly a company that gets me speaking jobs. There are many aspects to this business that the audience doesn't see. For instance, there is the design of the product. I have something to do with that but the actual final time planner, album cover design or order form is completed by Mike. Then there is the actual shipping of the product. The boxes, the packing materials, the tapes, the labels, or the post office runs. Then there is the promotion of the product called Danielle Kennedy. That is done through mailouts, by phone and sometimes by foot. It takes follow-up as well as the creation of new phone scripts. Then there is the actual typing up of the contracts and scheduling of airline flights, tickets, connections, return of contracts, processing of product orders, mail orders of books, bookkeeping, and profit and loss statements. Claudette Albert, our coordinator, does a fine job assisting Michael and I with all of that. Then there is the whole creative side of the work. I must design new workbooks for my programs, write books, and create scripts for new audio tapes and video training systems.

As one of the owners of Danielle Kennedy Productions, I have made it my business to do every job known to me that occurs in this company. At some point, I have packed boxes and brought shipments to the post office and airport. I have trained our coordinator on how to do itineraries and work with executive officers in various states. Why? Because I am out selling Danielle Kennedy and what she means in the training field. I better know how every part of this organization works. If someone says will your time planner hold up? What is it made of? I better respond with "Absolutely. It's made of Velcro. It's washable. I have already put mine in the washing machine and dryer. And here are the colors you can get it in."

One of the biggest problems companies face today is that they put people in the field that do not know how every department back at the home office works. These salespeople find themselves handling an objection by promising to give the moon. "Oh you need this product in three days. No problem (whenever I hear this expression I worry). We can have it hand-carried to your door in three days." Then of course they go back to the company and find out the product is on back order for three months. Had they been familiar with the problems and facets of each department they could have handled that objection with the **It's Worth the Wait Script:**

"This product is the hottest item in our line right now. As a matter of fact, I can't possibly get you a shipment before early July. But you will be getting the first shipment that comes off the truck. You are gonna love it. And believe me, you will realize then it was worth the wait."

Each salesperson is like a pebble that drops in the water and causes a ripple or special effect. Make sure you are not causing unnecessary tidal waves. Know your company, product and all department functions.

EIGHT NATURAL REACTIONS PEOPLE EXPERIENCE WHEN THEY DECIDE TO BUY

Most people getting ready to decide on a product or service go through some very normal, natural reactions. The item and how it can injure his or her pocketbook determines the length of time it will take an individual to go through each feeling. It can take anywhere from a split second to a year, or in some extreme cases a lifetime. An example of a lifetime might be the busy executive who always wanted a boat to go fishing. At 65, he buys the boat and wonders what took him so long.

1. *Exploration.* Buyers begin exploring for a product or service half aware of what their needs are but open to all possibilities and options when they first begin the search. Don't goof up by becoming discouraged when negative comments come up this early in the confrontation between you and the customer. Just converse naturally about your product. You are helping them explore possibilities. It's too early to worry if they'll buy or not. You don't even know their needs.

2. *Slight withdrawal.* A few folks react enthusiastically from the outset about a new idea or product but most refrain from early excitement. Keep in mind that early reaction with customers involves a lot of past life experiences, basic personalities, backgrounds, parental influence and financial viewpoints. They may not even hear what you are really saying yet. They may only know that they are moving into new territory. Their inner life (reactions of their mind and emotions) is all they are hearing. Keep that in mind when you sense slight withdrawal. Watch: "We aren't even sure we need to look at this computer right now. We are a growing company but we may not have quite the workload one needs to rationalize a new complicated system." Or: "My wife's expecting and an additional bedroom may be in order. But then again we might add on. I don't know!" Remain enthusiastic and just keep talking sunny side up. Lots of benefits. They are merely mouthing expressions of ignorance due to lack of information. After your initial positive approach, if you are sensing slight withdrawal, remember what I said earlier about not going wild with enthusiasm in the beginning. It just scares them. Remain confident and positive.

3. *Raise their level of awareness and shut up.* During the interview, all your questions and product knowledge serve the buyers. It raises their level of awareness of why they are there. Lots of pauses in between questions and answers are okay. Let them stare into space. It's all sinking in. Allow their own light bulbs to go off. Bring in the candle but let them light it. Keep the fun going. "You mentioned weekend quests. It's hard to believe this sofa is actually a roll-out queen-sized bed. Most couch-beds have no exterior style. Check this design." Then demonstrate and don't say a word. If this couch really looks more like a piece from a designer group, telling them it's a bed will be surprise enough. At this point, their desire will grow. Don't jump on every so-called objection they have. They still may be self-talking and again they don't know enough about the benefits of this product yet. You could lose them fast if you talk too much.

4. *More questions and interest.* "So this sofa is actually less expensive than the couch that doesn't convert to a bed?" Now you can tell that their need and interest is growing because they ask

verification questions. This is a sure sign. "Just to be sure I understood, did you say if we decide to purchase now, the price holds for 30 days?" Don't go into orbit with enthusiasm when these verification questions happen. I know you are sitting there thinking, "Yippee, it's going to fly." But *cool way down.* You could scare them at this point.

5. *Deliberate pondering.* We know now it's looking good, but beware. If you think you are getting nervous imagine your buyers. How do they react at this serious stage? Usually negatively. Lots of so called objections. They are thinking out loud again. Please keep that in mind. And the more they *deliberately ponder* the sale, the more comments. Of course, the pro feels like he is close to a sale and when a negative comment is made we feel like all is lost. *Don't panic.* Let anything happen. Be confident in yourself and your product.

6. *More doubt, questions and anxiety.* The only thing you do at this time is answer specific questions. "What happens if it breaks down in 45 days? Is there a warranty?" Just answer, shut up and listen.

7. *Finalizing and resolving doubt.* Almost there. Customer says, "If I take it home and we don't like it can I return it within 24 hours and get credit on my charge?"

8. *Locking it up.* Even when all the objections have been handled and you have done a great job interviewing and demonstrating, a call for action is necessary. Why? Because most of us need assistance and guidance when purchasing. Check the closing chapter for specific scripts and details.

SIX WAYS TO REMOVE THE STING
FROM ANY AND ALL OBJECTIONS

These all go hand in hand with the eight natural reactions customers have.

1. *Remember self-talk is good.* People that are interested and excited do this. If they could care less, they wouldn't say a word. Take some of the sting away by just sitting still and proceeding as

planned with your presentation. Hey—you are revving these people up. Relax and have some fun, you mover and shaker, you.

2. *Listen twice.* When a question or objection comes up the second time, get into it with the customer and talk it out. "Danny, I don't like the idea of buying a product I haven't seen in person. I can't buy from just a catalog." Repeat to them what they just said. Maybe your product is very saleable through brochures and the need is there for the customer but somewhere in the person's background, a family member told him to "handle the goods before buying." Keep in mind that if other comments only come up once you don't need to satisfy the comment. But this is the second time around, so you must analyze this with your people. Encourage them to discuss why they feel this way. Never act like they are silly for feeling the way they do. Make it safe. Repeat to the buyer, *"Under ordinary circumstances purchasing a product by catalogue scares people doesn't it?"* Then listen. Then add, *"Unfortunatly we don't have the space to stock the inventory here but the low percentage of returns on this item after delivery, during the last 25 years, has made it a crowdpleaser sight unseen. However, if this is a real problem for you, I do know of two local satisfied customers who took delivery this month. I could call them and see if we could drop in and see the product."* Now that you have that customer in a happy mood, we can proceed to the next objection or crisis.

3. *Allow any problem to come up.* New people are so afraid. I was. We talk constantly, thinking customer's mere questions are presenting a problem. The naturals with experience know how different people's tastes and personalities are. They figure they don't have all the answers, so sometimes, they will have to admit, *"I am not sure about that question but I have some excellent sources to tap. I'll be back in x number of minutes with an intelligent solution, hopefully."*

4. *Never say, "Have to."* "We have to" scares the customer. If you come across with an attitude of being very disappointed if this sale doesn't fly, they'll wonder who you are more interested in. Them or you? We should always live and communicate:

"If this doesn't fit your needs, we aren't going to push you into it. I want the best solution for you, Mr. Customer."

No one has to buy anything and you don't have to sell anything. We do it because everyone benefits. Often, if you come across like this, it will have the opposite effect on the customer. Customer thinks, "I like this guy. But I want him to realize I don't want to start looking all over again. I want to buy this thing. I hope he knows I'm serious." As a salesperson, always remember, you *are not trapped*. You have other customers, interviews and appointments in your bright future. Keep a good perspective and at the same time concentrate with your whole heart and soul on what's best for the customer in front of you.

5. *Don't take it personally.* Remember to disconnect feelings from buyer's objections. And from the buyer's excitement. Keep cool. They go up and down and you'll be exhausted if you match every feeling they feel. One of my faults is getting too excited too soon. If I think I am coming close to a big order, engagement, or interview , I act like Bill Cosby on one of his T.V. commercials. He is talking to someone on the phone. They are giving him good news. He covers his hand over the phone and starts mouthing words of excitement and rolling his eyes. He's trying to tell the person in the room something great may happen. Don't send any balloons up yet. Wait until it is for sure. No matter how hard I try, this is a tough one for me when I am excited.

6. *Keep an objection notebook.* I began my sales career without any training. Sometimes a super natural script would flow out of my mouth and I'd wonder, "Where did that come from?" When I lost sales, I would beat myself over the head because of the wrong things that were said. But when I made a sale with a natural script, I'd lose sight of those words in the happiness of the moment.

Then, one day, I said to myself: "Wait a minute. I want to examine what didn't work, so I can avoid saying the same thing again. But it's got to be even more important to study what did work so I'll be sure to repeat my most effective scripts whenever I can."

From then on, after a selling session I'd replay the whole thing in my mind. First, I would search my mind for the sets of words, body language and staging that had worked well at overcoming objections and I'd write all of those things down.

Only after searching for the good things, would I go over my mistakes and omissions and the things that hadn't worked very well. But instead of worrying about my blunders, I simply worked at coming up with better ideas to overcome each objection. Every time I thought of something, I would write it down. You'll find that it's amazing what brilliant ideas you'll have—after it's too late for that particular sale.

But it isn't too late to gain an important benefit from any sale that got away. By writing down what you should have said and memorizing your brilliant response, what will instantly pop into your mind the next time you face that objection? Your super natural script.

Searching your mind for lessons after every attempt to sell will yield valuable hints for future use whether that particular attempt was successful or not. In every sales position, certain objections keep coming up over and over. That's a huge plus for you because repeat objections are ones you can become very skillful at overcoming. And let's face it, without problems, objections and barriers, there would be no need for the salesperson.

CHAPTER **7**

NATURAL WAYS TO
NEGOTIATE

Peace at Any Price ✦ *Exchange* ✦ *Take Off Your
Slippers* ✦ *Be Human* ✦ *Don't Take a Hard and
Fast Position* ✦ *What Is Your Negotiating
Posture?* ✦ *Separate the Person from the
Problem* ✦ *Watch How You Use Scarcity* ✦ *Self-
Image of All Parties Is Important* ✦ *Air Emotions
Out* ✦ *Get Off the Defensive* ✦ *Communication Is the
Key* ✦ *Try Letting Go* ✦ *Make It Safe*

My niece Susan has started an interesting new career. It is called
"divorce mediation." She has decided to take her degree in psy-
chology and use it to teach people how to problem solve and
negotiate at the time of divorce. She will show individuals how
emotions can have a drastic effect on a problem that has to be
solved. Negotiating at the bargaining table is a lot less explosive
than negotiating at the divorce courts, but both situations require
similar skills.

PEACE AT ANY PRICE

Let's use divorce again as an example. One is the so-called easy-
going person who just wants the whole situation over with. If
they have instigated the divorce and there is a third party waiting
in the wings, sometimes their guilt causes them to want out fast
and quick. Because they feel they have injured the other spouse,
they are sometimes willing to walk away with nothing just to
appease their guilt. The problem is never that just one person is

responsible for a divorce. Sometimes the so-called underdog has done some mean maneuvers for years to get the situation to the point it's at. No one person should take full blame for the problem and try to make up for their so-called madness through money. Later the "peace at any price" people will go off like bombs when they finally understand that they gave up too much. I have seen very generous people in older years get quite stingy because they are now overreacting to the years that they felt people took advantage of them.

As a salesperson, keep in mind that whenever you are involved with more than one party, in any type of negotiation, there may be one who is more of a "pushover" than the other. There may be one party who wants "peace at any price" just to get the negotiations over with. Perhaps his or her whole life has been a hassle, when it came to any type of negotiation. As a kid, older brothers or sisters always got what they wanted because this person gave in. As an adult that same format has followed. This type of person must be taught exchange. He or she must be taught how right and enjoyable exchange is. And they must bleep the past out of their mind, which is telling them: "Oh, you are negotiating again. That means you are going to get the rotten end of the deal."

EXCHANGE

Let's imagine for a moment that my parents were very wealthy and I grew up in an environment of total luxury and affluence. As a child it didn't matter what I wanted, I got it. My world was sunshine, lollipops and rainbows, and I just assumed that everything I needed or wanted would be provided. I never had hard times. Then suddenly as an adult things begin to change. My father loses all his money in the stock market and my mother passes away. I have no job skills because all my life I had been provided for by my rich heritage. Now my father is poverty stricken and sick and he asks me for shelter and support. I turn on him. I see him as an obnoxious fool who never should have let all his money get eaten up in the stock market. I tell him I have my own life now and my goal is to find a rich man who can replace the lifestyle he has blown for me because of his stupid decision making. Sound ludicrous? Not really. There are people who feel they are "owed" something. Why? Because from the time they have been very young, they have been out of exchange with people. And their parents taught them this. Now what does that mean? It means that when someone gives and gives and never learns to take, or when someone takes and takes and never learns to give, he or she does not have a fair exchange with people. Basically, this does not bring happiness.

We have dear friends who are always making sure that the exchange is going correctly with the four of us. In the beginning, we thought that was a bit peculiar but we have found that the relationship is great and not full of resentments. For instance, if we took them to dinner last week, they will buy this week. You may say, "How petty!" Fine, say that, but we all get along and no one ever feels taken advantage of. When you make an effort to be sure that you have given something of yourself back to a person who has helped you, it creates a wonderful balance in your life.

Right now I am thinking about my friend and pal, Tom Hopkins. If Joan Rivers were writing this, she would talk about Johnny Carson. Both of these men have had profound influences on our careers. Joan tells the story of how everyone thought she was a horrible comic except Carson. He put her on his show and promoted her career for the last 20 years. Tom Hopkins is one of the greatest sales trainers and lecturers in the world. He took me out of the ranks and promoted me because of his belief in my talent. He talked about me and sold audiences on me day after day for years. He is still doing it. He opened up many doors for me. I will never be able to give him that type of exchange in return. He already had the fame and success in his field. But a way that I can keep a good exchange in is to thank him and acknowledge him publicly as much as possible and continue developing my talents. I know how much he believes in my talent. If I got lazy, I would be making a liar out of him. So that's how we keep our exchange in. He keeps bragging and I keep trying to get better.

Now, let's go back to the example of the child who gets the world handed to her. A parent and a child have a similar exchange problem as Tom and I have (also Carson and Rivers). There is no way a kid can ever pay back a parent for all the neat things they have done. I think about my mom and dad. The educational and recreational opportunities alone that I have had because of my parents are too much to comprehend. But I have kept the exchange in by never letting them down. I took every opportunity they gave me and ran with it. *Keeping the exchange in with people nurtures relationships.* Mom and I get along great but she knows I don't expect anything from her. Therefore, when she gives, I know she enjoys it. And she is learning to let me, now that I can, give to her also. Give what? Myself, my time or money. It doesn't matter what it is.

Let's say you are well off and have a friend whom you have known and loved your whole life but he is broke. How do you feel when he hits you up for money? Uncomfortable? Maybe at some low point in your life he gave to you and now you have a chance to help him. That means that you are in exchange. But if you have always been the giver and he has always been the taker, you are going to get pretty sick of the expectant attitude on his part. I see that a lot with friends. Maybe some high-income people have some middle-to low-income friends. The struggling friends expect the affluent ones to buy dinner all the time. Why? "Well, they can afford it," is the comment you will often hear. So what? Just because by some stroke of fate or hard work this person has money, does that mean that all their friends are entitled to free lunches and meals for the rest of their born days? I think people who are well off enjoy going out with people who sometimes pay and sometimes don't, just like the rest of the world.

What does this all have to do with negotiation? If you and I first understand the principle of exchange, then I think negotiation in the sales field, or any field for that matter, will be a lot easier. People like to have a fair exchange between them. Therefore, the point of all negotiation should be *fair exchange*. Keep in mind that outsiders may not think the exchange looks fair, but the parties have set up some kind of silent agreeement. (Parents and kids or Carson and Rivers: "If you are being the best you can be, I'm happy.") If I am acting as a mediator between parties as a salesperson or if I am just mediating between myself, my company and the product, I must keep in mind that *no one likes to feel taken advantage of and ripped off.* Everyone likes to feel that they have given a little and taken a little too. That's what fair exchange is all about.

Also remember this with all the folks you hire. Sometimes secretaries feel out exchange with their bosses. They are being paid to type but they also run kids around, clean the office and have added a million chores that weren't part of the deal. You may say, "C'mon, Mary loves to do that and go the extra mile." That may be so but if you do not reward her or acknowledge her, sooner or later, it will catch up with you. Either she will do it and talk behind your back or quit. That is because the exchange is not fair between you. Please don't think I expect everyone to sit around with a tally sheet. "Well it must be your turn to do this or that. I did it last week." Just be aware of what exchange is. Also be aware of that sinking feeling you get when you feel you have been taken advantage of. Connect up the two things: exchange and being taken advantage of. I would rather have you admit to someone that you feel a bit used, then have you walk around smiling when you are ready to kill inside. That's called *suppression.* Now let's see how this all applies to the customers.

TAKE OFF YOUR SLIPPERS

I cannot tell you the importance of having empathy during negotiations. Please try to take off your slippers and step into the shoes of the other person involved in the negotiation. Don't get stuck with just your viewpoint. Don't think you are always right. I can't stand people who are so blind (with eyes no less) that they can only see their way. And it seems these people should be more empathetic because they have done some horrible things in their life and yet haven't learned a thing from the lesson. As a matter of fact, they are downright brutal to their friends who have made the same mistakes they have made. One thought I have had about life: "Never say never." You could find yourself in "Never, Never

Land" after you vowed you would never make the same stupid mistake so and so made. Most important, when negotiating for peace, prosperity, a car or furniture, remember: As a salesperson, don't look down your nose at the customer who is struggling with a problem regarding the purchase. Make it okay for them to feel that way and let them air out. They need human understanding.

BE HUMAN

All through this book, I have been telling you to be the natural and the pro. Be prepared. Strut your stuff at the interview and the presentation. Handle each objection as it comes up. But please, first and foremost, be human. While you are negotiating, use basic down-to-earth examples to plead your case. I can't help but think of my old real estate days when sometimes two or three of us would present an offer from our individual buyer on a seller's property. I can remember feeling my skin crawl as some sales-people would present their offer to the seller. "Well, Mr. Seller, you have a lovely home but. . . my people don't like blue carpet, my people don't like gold drapes, on and on, and this is going to cost a fortune to replace. So, when we created this offer, we had to keep all of these things in our mind for negotiation." Then boom they would tell the price. By then the homeowner was ready to kill the salesperson, thinking, "How dare that idiot talk about my beautiful property that way. My wife made those gold drapes. I wouldn't sell this house to that fool if I was on skid row and needed a dime from anywhere." Other times, I would go out on an offer to present a contract and salespeople would sit there and tell the seller how much the family loved his home. And what a coincidence it was because they had a daughter the same age as their daughter, etc., etc. . . And that homeowner would glow. That homeowner would be thinking, "Boy, I sure would like to see these people get the house. They are so nice." It pays to re-member that people's emotions are at stake when you negotiate. Be ever so careful. Treat with loving care.

DON'T TAKE A HARD AND FAST POSITION

When negotiating, it is better to say to yourself, "I want this agreement to work." Don't say, "By God, either this goes my way or it ain't going." I have seen salespeople take a position for their customers and do their customers a terrible injustice. Their customers really wanted to purchase the article or service, but the salesperson had given them some advice about a certain position they should take. In the long run, the customer didn't get the product and therefore the salesperson was not paid his fee or commission. Plus the salesperson should not be making up the customer's mind.

Another place I see this happen a lot is in divorce. The two ex-spouses begin arguing and taking a position over something and the children get hurt. They get hurt because both parties said, "I want to get my way. If I don't get my way then everybody is going to lose." And guess who loses—the kids. No agreement is made and the child suffers. I will admit, when you are dealing with a person on the other side of the negotiation who takes a position all the time and is constantly backing you into a corner, it is difficult to not take a position yourself. The best solution I have found is to refuse to negotiate with such disagreeable, hard core individuals. Let them play a game with someone else who understands their style.

Now I hear you saying, "What if I have to negotiate with these idiots. I can't walk away, Danny. I have no choice. My boss says it has to be done. It means a big order for myself and family. What do I do?" Then don't stoop to their positional style. No matter how hard core they are stay honest, calm, direct and nonmanipulative. Example: "Gee, I'd love to buy it but my wife won't let me." (Good guy–bad guy routine and you are the salesperson.) This is a tactic that a lot of husbands and wives use to keep salespeople off their backs. They have an unspoken agreement that one is the bad guy. "Gee, I am a helpless victim. I'd love to rush into this but my wife ain't one to tamper with." Before anything can be done with this type of situation, the salesperson has to find out whether or not the so-called good guy really wants the product or just doesn't have the guts to say no, and is using the spouse as an out. If you find motivation there, then proceed to work with the so-called bad guy (the wife). "There is nothing worse than a salesperson pushing something down your throat. I do not intend to do that. But your spouse tells me this product is a must for you and your family. How do you feel about it?" Then begin finding out if the objections are too major to overcome and what, if anything, can be done about it. I would even directly ask the bad guy, "Are you usually the final say in all the decisions? Should I just deal directly with you, seeing how your spouse indicates that he wants it but you need more information?" This sometimes puts them in an uncomfortable position. If the so-called good guy really doesn't want the merchandise, the truth comes out at times like this from the other spouse. "You know it's funny, but if he wants it, it's fine with me but I think it's just his way of saying no gracefully."

If you have a boss to report to, then you at least can look him or her straight in the eye and say, "I am trying to deal as directly and honestly as possible with these people but they have an un-spoken game going." Then if you need to call in your superior to meet the folks, the superior may back you up with "If our product doesn't fit into both of your lifestyles, perhaps just you, Mr. Good Guy, may want to purchase it." What this does is bring the subject to a head. "Hey, wait a minute," the so-called good guy may say, "I didn't agree to anything like that." You have pulled the lie and now can walk away with dignity. Or else that person who really wants it may take a stand in order to save face and purchase the product. But I have watched too many people negotiate with game players and it just isn't fair to the salespeople. Salespeople do not deserve the treatment they sometimes get.

WHAT IS YOUR NEGOTIATING POSTURE?

This is an important question to ask yourself. Do you want to negotiate to the point of losing a friend, long-term relationship or contract? Is this the type of issue that ought to be dropped? Does your backing down show that you aren't going to major in the minors and aim to please the customer? Or does it indicate that you can be taken for a ride? I think you have to look at the history you have with the folks on the other side of the table. If they have understood the word *exchange* in the past and you are looking like a real cad here, then I would back down. If, once again, they are trying to railroad you, then risk the relationship because it may not be that healthy to you and your company in the long run. These are questions only you can answer but I want to make sure you are aware of them. Sometimes, emotions get so steamed up, after matters have settled down, we wonder why we went off the deep end with this position to such valued customers. But it is too late. We did it now and there is nothing left to do but move in a different direction.

SEPARATE THE PERSON FROM THE PROBLEM

When negotiating, never ever get personal. If you need to educate or make a point, in an area where the other side is either naive or misinformed, use yourself as an example. Try this script:

"This situation came up with me once when Marilyn and I were buying a computer. One of the ideas we had was that the salesperson would know exactly how to operate the software when it was delivered. We didn't realize a technician from another department had to be commissioned to come over and handle that side of the transaction. I can see how you want that included in the price but, like me, you are figuring in the technical additions into this price and they tell me it can't be done."

So much better to use yourself to explain than this: "Do you have any idea (you fool) what it costs to get a technician out here to get this software in operation? Our company would go broke if we gave this type of service away." Bad, bad, bad. Never give the party the idea that they are stupid. We must separate the problem from the parties at all times.

WATCH HOW YOU USE SCARCITY

Let's say that a person wants to buy a box of nails. However, there is only one place in town that has the kind of nails he needs. He goes there, buys the nails and is told that he will have to wait five days for delivery because they are out of the nails right now. The owner of the store and the customer agree on a price and the customer pays in advance. When the customer goes to pick up the nails the salesperson uses this on him: "I had to get the nails from a different location. This cost me $5.OO extra so I must raise the price on these nails." Understand I am using a crazy example because normally in a store with marked prices you are protected from this. A lot of times, when you buy elsewhere, you are not protected. The customer feels trapped and taken under the above circumstances. The salesperson has broken agreement and hit him up for another $5.OO. Recently, we had a similar situation happen with a landscape man working on our front yard. He gave us a bid and then came back crying the blues because the lights under the tree were a lot more expensive than he quoted. We didn't say a word. He knew we weren't falling for it. His comment, after our silence was, "Well, I guess it is my problem and I'll have to eat the difference." You better believe it. I can't tell you the number of times I made promises to customers and something extra came up which I hadn't figured in. I swallowed it, knowing that if you are ethical, once the agreement is made, it is made. Stick to the agreements.

SELF-IMAGE OF ALL PARTIES IS IMPORTANT

Have you ever noticed that an agreement sometimes gets made and the negotiating parties never stop arguing long enough to realize it? Because one party took a position early on in the negotiations, things have come to a standstill. They do not know how to gracefully get off the position they put themselves into. Help them. I can remember, when we started our speaking business, making a hard and fast policy that the speaker would only fly first class. This was stated at the time because of our narrow point of view. The speaker speaks all day and flies all night. Sometimes, over the years, the speaker had been plopped in the middle of two burly individuals and couldn't even rest her arm for five hours. When the speaker arrived home, it took three days to detangle her pretzel-like body from discomfort. The speaker's manager and husband said, "No way will the speaker go through discomfort like this again." Hurray for the manager but as time went on we realized the budgetary problems companies have. Here we are worried about the speaker being cramped up. Every extra nickel the company who is thinking of hiring us has this month is going for outside speakers to educate their people. So, we changed the rule. But we said things like, "The job of our president is to make sure the speaker is always feeling great for the betterment of the program being presented. So depending on circumstances, we reserve the right to request first class." That way, the president of the speaking company saves face when he changes policy on airfares. It's so important to let all parties walk away from the negotiation table with their heads held high.

AIR EMOTIONS OUT

There is absolutely nothing wrong with letting people get stuff off their chest when negotiating. "Every darn time we buy something either they can't get it to us on time or the price has just gone up." The best thing a salesperson can do is listen and also acknowledge that customer. "I know how you feel. My husband and I just bought a capuccino machine last week and we couldn't figure out how to get it started. When we did get it going it leaked all over, so we had to return it to the store." Make your examples real, so they can also see you can be a frustrated human being at times like this. And it is okay. But let them talk and talk because you will find that they just want a sympathetic ear. Plus negotiating almost always brings out the emotions in people.

GET OFF THE DEFENSIVE

When the objections are flying during the negotiations don't get touchy and defensive. Welcome advice and criticism. "Do I really act like it bothers me when you bring up the poor packaging? Actually, I feel embarrassment because I never thought it would leave the warehouse that way. Let's figure out ways to correct this problem." When you get on the defensive, everyone around you either does the same thing or thinks you are a bullhead. They would just as soon communicate with someone else about the matter than you. Don't be afraid of criticism and advice. If you know what you are doing, you and the product will weather all storms. But if you are insecure, being defensive is the sure symptom of that ailment.

COMMUNICATION IS THE KEY

If you know how to communicate your ideas clearly and concisely, negotiations are always easier. That means you keep good eye contact with the individuals you are talking with and your body language reflects confidence and security. Watch your posture. Don't slump and look dejected during negotiations. Sit up straight, get a lot of rest beforehand and use the following four elements in good communication to get your points across.

1. **Purpose:** *What is my purpose during this negotiation?* Do I have a good true purpose? Do I want the greatest good for individuals involved? Do I want them to take the product back to their offices, factories, or homes and be thrilled that they made such a good investment? Is my purpose pure?

2. **Attention:** *Do I have the attention of the people I am negotiating with?* Or are they somewhere else mentally but physically sitting in the room? Do I have a bona fide, qualified and well-interviewed customer in front of me or am I communicating with someone who is a user or a manipulator? Have I lost their attention because of my own lack of enthusiasm and pzazz? Do I know the product

and does my presentation have a true natural flow and glow? What can I do to get their attention back on the subject and negotiation at hand?

3. Satisfaction: *When we are negotiating, customers should get satisfaction from the salesperson each time they make an important statement or request.* "It's important that we get delivery by Christmas," says the customer. The salesperson must satisfy the customer by repeating exactly what the customer just said in the form of a question, showing no emotion. "Is it important that you get delivery by Christmas?" That way the customer knows that someone has been listening to what he has to say. Too many times, during the negotiation, customers feel like no one heard a thing they have said. Give customers the satisfaction of knowing you have heard them. Repeat it to them with clarity, sometimes in the form of a question.

4. Acknowledgment: *"I understand how important pre-Christmas delivery is to you."* This doesn't necessarily say you can pull it off but it shows that you acknowledged their request, at least. I think it is so important to be human first and the salesperson second.

TRY LETTING GO

The worst thing the salesperson can do during negotiations is panic. "Yes, but you said that if I got this to the store today you would buy it." When you panic you in turn panic the customers who begin to wonder. They think, "Are they interested in me being satisfied with this product or do they care more about their own pocketbook and buck?" As I have told you throughout this whole book, there is nothing wrong with the take-away. Not everyone is going to purchase your product, nor should they. If they suddenly get into a panic towards the conclusion of the purchase and indicate they have had second thoughts, listen to those thoughts. Try this:

"I see you are upset. What is bothering you? Your satisfaction over this product is more important to me than the money earned on this.

*If it isn't right for you, we aren't going to do it. As a matter of fact, I
won't let you do something under pressured or forced conditions. Can
we talk? Open up and tell me what's bothering you."*

Now could it happen that you lose the sale? Sure it has happened to me many times. But the customer relationships I have
built up are very important. As a matter of fact, I probably lost a
lot of sales in that present moment but the future held triple the
business because of that lost sale. Why? Because the people appreciated the honesty and gave me more future referrals than I
could handle.

MAKE IT SAFE

If your negotiations are not going well, keep in mind that perhaps
you never earned the right to negotiate for the customer back in
the interviewing stages. That's when you become a safe connection
for your customers. If you have truly shown them by word and
action that you know what you are doing, they won't be afraid
to let their defenses down a bit during the critical negotiation
period of selling. More than anything people want to feel "safe"
in your hands. Safe from what? Safe from harm. That's right.
Usually, we think of just bodily harm but do you realize the mental
and emotional harm that happens between people. When customers are buying ten dollars or ten thousand dollars worth of
merchandise, it is a bit of a stress to them and it is so important
to feel that it is okay. You are the doctor, the nursemaid, the
psychologist, the adviser and the good ear to your customers.
Always keep that dignified and ethical posture in your customers
eyes.

When negotiating try thinking about the emotional issue of
divorce. Think of all the kids that have gotten mentally harmed
because their parents weren't in safe hands when negotiating.
Neither parent could count on the other one for respect, dignity
and safety of feelings presented in the other's environment. Though
selling is not like divorce court, the same sets of people and sen-
sitivities are brought into the light. And the natural knows the
price one pays in order to always be "right."

CHAPTER **8**

CLOSING CUSTOMERS, NATURALLY!

Sales-Killer Questions a Natural Would Never Ask ◆ *The Either/Or Solution* ◆ *Super Natural Scripting:*
> *Tell the Story; Sell the Painting; You're Gonna Love It and Me Script; I Own This Product Too Script; Who Can Never Be Sure Script; Confidence Close; The Deadline Script; I Am Afraid So Just Do It Script; I Know You Are Dying to Try This Script; Let's Assume; Is It Really Smart to Wait?; The Cabbage Patch Story; The Pros/Cons Script; The Dollar Is It Script; I Hope We Have It/or I Can Get It Script; Only the Chosen Ones Script*

Believe it or not, most super natural salespeople don't like the easy close. As a matter of fact, the game of life is the same way. When things appear to be going too smoothly, we always try to roughen up the waters a bit. Human beings like some barriers in their way to make things interesting to overcome. We may squawk and carry on but basically we love the challenge. In this chapter, I want you to act like closing customers is a game. You have certain freedoms with these customers. But there are certain barriers that have to be overcome before the sale is made.

As a new salesperson, the thing I hated to do most was call for a decision from a customer. I enjoyed building rapport and becoming friends but I always hoped they would just buy the thing on their own. I actually created my first sale by accident. I had shown the couple several homes. They finally found *the* home. I was so dumb I didn't pick up the buying signs. We had just left the house for the second time and we were in the car on the way

129

back to the office. The scene went something like this: I was driving the car and the couple were in the back seat. They tapped me on the shoulder and said: "Danny, we want it." I replied, "You want what?" Dumb, Dumb, Dumb. They answered, "We want the home." To which I replied, "Don't you want to think it over?" I wanted them to think it over because I didn't know how to fill out the paperwork. I needed a week in the bathroom with the door locked to bone up on the figures and forms. But in spite of me, they did buy. I definitely was my own worst enemy.

Closing was the most difficult aspect of my business. It really didn't have to be that way. I was great at interviewing and really knew my product well. I should have relaxed and done my thing. But it took a long time. Part of my problem was feeling like an intruder. The act of closing calls for some personal decisions between one or more individuals. It also involves people's checkbooks and quite frankly I never liked discussing money.

As a child, we never talked about money. My dad's income was a mystery to me. Money still makes me feel uncomfortable. I know a lot of you are the same way. The natural is usually very sensitive to people and doesn't want to offend or hurt their feelings. There are ways you can overcome this. I did. So can you.

Keep in mind that you have a goal with every customer that comes your way—to close them on your product. Decision-causing is another name for selling. You are the factor that promotes some type of change with your customers. Don't ever forget that. Please don't feel guilty about it. Helping people make a decision about something that can benefit them in their life is good. Repeat after me: Closing is good. Change is often good. It is critical that you believe what you are doing for the customer is good. If you do not feel that way please get out of the field. I have heard salespeople say to me, "I feel like I am ripping people off. Plus inside I feel I am making too much money."

The world of the super natural star should be a peaceful, contented world. The conscience should be clear. Naturals know that our economy runs best when sales are up and people are buying. I love to buy. Don't you? Some creators say, "Don't sell it, I just want to create it." That's selfish. If you have a talent and can contribute to the world through the beauty and practicality of your creation, why not let people buy it? Look at Michael Jackson, for example. What a waste of talent that would have been if the world couldn't listen to his *Thriller* or *Off the Wall* album. If Michael didn't let the promoters market his stuff, I personally would have lost. He motivates me to dance, write, cook and live. His talent is a gift to the world. Thanks Michael for letting someone sell you to the world. Thanks for letting me buy your records. Keep making products. We want to buy your stuff. If that creation makes you even richer, God bless you.

I know of a whole family who don't feel a bit guilty about strutting their stuff to the consumer. It's the Mayer family. Their mother, Ruth, (she has nine children) is the artist and the family members are the super natural salespeople. They sell mom's creations at the Ruth Mayer Gallery in Laguna Beach, California. Recently, she finished a painting of Santa Catalina Island that took over a year to make. One Christmas the silkscreens of the original (250) were being offered to the first comers for $1200 a piece. Her sons weren't ashamed to tell you they sold 120 silkscreens. There were only 130 left by the day before Christmas. They believe in her work so much they can't imagine people not wanting to beautify their homes with a Ruth Mayer original. The family tells the customers about Ruth, the artist. They have scripts about who owns her things and past clients that love her work.

I call them scripts because I am sure they have repeated the same message over and over. To each customer, it sounds like the first time. Why? Because they are naturals and love selling something they believe in. I call the classical things naturals say to the customer to help them make a decision *scripts*. A good play has a script (even a bad play does, so watch it). This keeps the flow going and the players must know their lines. If they can't deliver, you won't sit through the performance. Closing is also that way.

Besides scripts, knowing how to ask proper questions should not end at the interview. Questions should continue to be asked all the way through the closing sequence. The questions you ask and how you ask them is quite critical. Let's first look at some negative ways of asking and then move on to the more positive.

Later in the chapter, we will give you some super natural scripts to help the customer through the transition to ownership of your product.

SALES-KILLER QUESTIONS
A NATURAL WOULD NEVER ASK

There is one statement I have seen so-called salespeople make to a customer and it's a killer from the start: "Just buy this stuff, buddy or get off my back." Let's go over some of the ways this rude intruder communicates this bad attitude to the customer.

> *"Do you want to get it?"* Horrible, but listen to the next rendition.

> *"Well, do you want to buy it or not?"* Even if they were going to go through with it, they won't now.

> *"Can I write you up for one?"* This isn't quite as bad, but the kill rate is about 6 out of 10.

No doubt, you are remembering all the push artists that tried some of those clever maneuvers on you. You are also thinking, "I hope I never ask killer questions like that." Well, you can definitely avoid it if you just think the plan and the script through a little bit before the performance. First thing to keep in mind is that those questions make not only the customer nervous but also the salesperson because they are so high risk. Either the customer is going to say yes or no. So, promise yourself right now never to ask yes/no type questions again.

My husband, Michael, tells me I am a constant closer. He will ask me where I want to go for dinner and I will reactively reply, "Where would you like to go, honey?" Of course, he does the same thing. We are both instinctive and natural salespeople. It has just become second nature. So, keep the following things in mind: When a customer asks you a question that demands a yes/no answer, try to answer it with a question. (*Customer:* "Do you think you can give me delivery on these awnings by December 17th? *Salesperson:* "Do you need delivery by the 17th?") Try this.

THE EITHER/OR SOLUTION

Almost any natural closing question can be worded to give the customer a set of choices or options. What I preach and teach are options. Never make customers feel trapped, but always give them the option to go one way or another. Listen:

> *"Would you prefer to pay with cash, credit card or check?"*
>
> *"Shall we bill this to your company or to you personally?"*
>
> *"Can I put a rush on this or would a standard two-week delivery be fine for you?"*
>
> *"Do you like the brown or the black?"*
>
> *"Do you think you would like the power of the larger engine or the economy of the smaller one?"*

The best thing about using questions is it makes the customer feel like they have a choice. Also, the more questions we ask and the more solutions we can come up with for the customer, the less they will feel in the dark.

One of the biggest changes people make in their life is moving. As a real estate salesperson, I had to constantly be aware of the stress the customer felt. When change occurs, buyers feel scared and in the dark. The good salesperson is continually taking the customer out of the dark and into a brighter place full of benefits. Major ticket items cause major stress to the buyer (houses, cars, furs, jewelry or artwork). Minor ticket items cause minor stress (books, cosmetics, cleaning products or record albums). The salesperson must learn strong, fact-filled scripts to handle major or minor closing decisions. This next section should get your own creativity going too. As you read some of my scripts, it should trigger some ideas for you to use with your situations and characters in your everyday play of selling.

SUPER NATURAL SCRIPTING

Tell the Story; Sell the Painting

Talking about Ruth Mayer, earlier in the chapter, reminded me of one of her excellent scripts she used with a customer to interest them in her Catalina painting. I call it, **Tell the Story; Sell the Painting.**

Oftentimes, the product itself is beautiful. But the story behind the product often enhances the beauty of the product. For instance, with Ruth Mayer's painting *Catalina,* it was a delight listening to her weave the story of the steps she took prior to its creation on canvas. Ruth is a pilot. One Christmas morning she was circling in the air above Avalon Bay, Santa Catalina Island. Her intention was to photograph the sight from the air. Then her year-long project of painting would begin. It was an ideal morning to photograph the bay. Hardly a cloud in the sky and every rooftop pointed towards the heavens. Ruth got what she wanted. For the next twelve months she created that picture on an easel with a palette knife, using over 120 different colors. She had me spellbound as she described the patience and talent that her *Catalina* drew from her in order to see the project to completion. I stood their gazing at that painting. I knew I had to have one.

It was funny but when I asked Ruth to share this story with me for my sales book, she cringed a little. Again, the word *sales* rubbed her the wrong way. She said, "I am not really thinking of the sale when I tell the story to the customer." I reassured her that I knew that. I also told her most super naturals do not think of the sale. They are too absorbed with the moment. But her story, whether she realized it or not, enhanced the sale.

You Are Gonna Love It and Me Script

If you have credibility in your customer's eyes, keep in mind how important it is to put your stamp of approval on the product and his decision to buy.

"You see Mr. Customer, I know You Are Gonna Love This and Me *once you've taken this product home and made it your own. I would not be saying this, if in good conscience, I didn't believe that this was right for you. Why? Well, in our business bad news travels fast. If you love the product, you will have no reason to complain. As a matter of fact, you will be telling all your friends how much you love it. If you buy this product and felt like you had been taken advantage of, you will let everyone in your world know that me and my product are the worst. Bad news travels much faster than good. I live where I work and my future reputation is at stake, as well as this sale. So, when I say,* You Are Gonna Love It, *I am really putting my reputation on the line."*

This script motivates buyers to say: "Let's do it. Write it up. How much of a deposit do I need?" The customer will often close you to sell it to them after this script. Why? Because you speak the truth. If it's wrong for them, they could ruin your reputation. They figure you are now taking part of the responsibility for this decision and it brings them relief. At the Ruth Mayer Gallery, they often give an opinion like, "You are gonna love this," as well as, "We want you to come back so we better not lead you astray." This holds a lot of credibility for me.

I Own This Product Too Script

Imagine that a car salesperson and you are chatting. You are trying to figure out what kind of a second car to get for your family. The car salesperson says ("me too"):

"I have teenagers too and I can honestly speak from experience on this one. I just bought our family this second car about six months ago. We are getting about 40 miles to the gallon. Can you believe it?"

Here is the human being talking, not just the salesperson. Please use personal experiences, as often as possible, in your presentation. What you are really saying to the customer is, *"Not only will I sell you this product, but I personally have stuck my neck and buck out and purchased the very same thing." What a natural!*

The Who Can Never Be Sure Script

Usually, people that are stalling to make a decision are worried about something. When they have self-confidence, they seem to buy readily. A buyer's self-confidence comes from a lot of factors. The salesperson's product knowlege and ability to determine the customer's needs count for plenty. You have to give customers all the information they need but some buyers are asking you to read a crystal ball. "What if unleaded gas isn't available in five years? What if convertibles go out of style? Will I be stuck with a lemon in ten years?" Believe me, most people don't get all perfect answers before they buy. Let's face it, only things that have already happened are knowable at this very second. This means that the knowable facts are the least of one's worries. The decisions that count are those that look forward to the unforseen future. We always predict the future. Some predictions have turned out to be great comedy material five years later. The best known economists in the country have been way off, after pouring over facts and figures daily. Every decision we have ever made is a hostage to fate. Make up a *Confidence Close*, similar to this, to handle the unforseen future with the worrier type customers.

"We never know what the future will bring and if we wait for it to happen, then it's too late to take advantage of today's opportunity. All of us examine the facts, make the best possible choices and proceed, don't you agree?"

Oftentimes, you can tell stories at this point (usually the customer will too.) "Remember when we put a down payment on our first car, Alice? The last $50.00 to our name. How about our first house? Can you believe we paid $10,555 for it and it's worth well over $60,000 today? Who would have believed that ten years ago?"

The Deadline Script

Open any printed material that comes to you in the mail and here's what you will see: "Order now to avoid disappointment." "Act now before it is too late." "This sale ends August 15th." "Offer void after September 10th." "This offer will never be repeated again."

You will rarely see a mass mailout that doesn't include a deadline close. Our son Kevin just wrote an ad to the local newspaper to try and sell his bike. We told him to write "Call Today" at the end of the ad. Building an urgent command is very important in selling. These words are effective. That's why everyone uses them.

Are you constantly on the lookout for *Deadline Closes?* You should be—they rank among the most effective methods known. A life insurance agent told me the first thing he wants to know about a prospect is his or her birthday. He has the prospect files set up by date so that he is reminded to call on people two weeks before their next birthday. Why? So he can say:

"Mr. and Mrs. Jones, I understand that Pete will be 40 in two weeks and rates will go up. But, if we put this policy through now, it will take the rate for age 39 and save you a lot of money. We need to get the application in right away to get it approved before Pete's next birthday."

This script works because it puts enough time pressure on people to break through their inertia. The natural close is the art of preventing postponement. Do you realize the number of people who depend on honest insurance and accounting people to keep their lives squared away? Hooray three times to these natural closers.

I'm Afraid, So Just Do It Script

Sometimes you have buyers who are indecisive and aren't sure whether they've bought or not. When I sold houses, I often reached this point with married couples. Both of them wanted the house but neither of them wanted to be the one to say yes. Neither wanted to say no either.

I understood how they felt. They had bought the house in every way except one—they hadn't broken through the paralyzing barrier of their indecision.

What did I do in those cases? I'd start filling out the order form and ask very reflexive type questions, such as address, telephone number or place of business. When the flow of responses had begun, I would calmly say, "This is just so we can keep everything together. If you decide to make an offer on this home, would you want them to leave the chandelier in the living room?"

Sometimes, it would be, ". . . would you want them to replace that broken tile in the kitchen?" There is always some little item you can ask about.

I'd proceed along that line, working up from minor details to crucial questions. "When would you want possession?" One of the last questions would be, "The larger the deposit, the more likely it is that our offer will go through. I suggest $3,000. Does that sound about right to you?"

Never ask indecisive people, "Do you want to purchase this piano?" If you organize your selling sequence right for this type of client, there's never any need to ask the hazardous *"Do you want it?"* question.

Between the time you start and finish filling out the order form, your indecisive buyers usually reconcile themselves to the fact that they have made the decision to buy. Of course, you must qualify your customers first. Make sure they want your product. Know that you have shown them your complete inventory and make sure what they want would best meet their needs and budget. Then there is no real reason why they should not go ahead and purchase your product.

I Know You Are Dying To Try This Script

They say salespeople are real suckers for other good salespeople. Boy, I sure am. When I see a pro in action, I just let them sell me

down the river. I know the product knowledge, confidence, courage, and affinity with people this takes. When I see a natural, I
want to watch every move. Not so long ago, I got taken down
the primrose path with the **I Know You Are Dying To Try
This Script.** My doorbell rang about five in the afternoon and
as usual about 12 kids and I answered the door. Everyone yelled
the usual, "I'll get it. It's for me." I opened the door and standing
there, with the biggest grin and widest pair of dark eyes I had
ever seen, was Andy, a black salesperson. Andy said: "Hey, how's
everyone doing today? I just came from your neighbors' houses—
Betty, Vicky and Jane. They thought you'd be dying to see this
too. I asked them, after they each bought a bottle, if I should take
it over to another neighbor's house and they said, by all means
that I should."

About then, I couldn't believe this kid. There I was, the sales
trainer herself with the eyes glued to Andy. He continued: "Have
you got some ketchup?" Short pause. Then: "Please get me some."
Of course, three kids ran to the refrigerator and got the ketchup.
He then proceeded to drip some on his shirt and rub it in. He took
out this bottle of cleaner and a rag, waited a few seconds and
rubbed it out. Then he said: "Have you got grease stains anywhere?" At that point, I was thinking of a million things for this
young man to do. "Yes," I said (along with 10 other kids yelling
with me). "The garage floor." He replied, "Let's hit it, Ms. Kennedy." We all marched into the garage. Lo and behold, the product
spoke for itself. All the grease came up. Then Andy went on with
such enthusiasm we all couldn't resist but fall in love with him.

*"How many kids do you have Ms. Kennedy? Oh brother! You need
my product. It really does the job. It works on clothes, floors, hub caps,
drains, and on and on. I know by now, if you are anything like Betty
and Vicky across the street, you are dying to try it."*

And of course, he wouldn't be back in the neighborhood again.
Well you guessed it, we bought and proceeded to talk about Mr.
Enthusiasm all through dinner. Daniel said to me, "Mom, Andy
made me die to try that stuff." What a natural . . .

The other thing we have to examine about Andy is his attitude.
The attitude of enthusiasm and assumption that you would be
dying for this when he got through with you. You can make this

part of your selling ability too. As long as people aren't down-right antagonistic, it can work. You need to be friendly, confident and well rehearsed with the scripts, questions and pauses. You must know your order form thoroughly because any hesitation in knowing what goes where is fatal to this approach. It's smooth, fast and you got it—natural!

In other words, you must be ready to make sales. If you are, why not make them faster and more often with the I Know You Are Dying to Try This Script?

Let's Assume Script

Take your friendly bottled water man. He's a salesperson. Every-time he comes over to take a bottle of empty water away, he replaces it. You may have three full bottles but he notices just the empty bottle. He never asks questions. He just walks in with a full bottle and walks out with an empty one. Few words are spoken but the message is the same—you just bought another bottle of water.

Is It Really Smart to Wait?

This script makes a lot of sense. Everything in my lifetime has never gotten cheaper to buy, only more expensive. Mickey Rooney said he bought a chocolate soda as a kid for five cents. Today, it costs at least $2.50. The only thing I know of that started out big and expensive and went down in price is the calculator. But most things, from a house to a bottle of hair spray, have gone up.

"Is It Really Smart to Wait? Think about things you bought 10 years ago. (Have them name a few items.) *Maybe your fur coat, your old car, your house, or that signed print from Norman Rockwell. What would it cost you to replace that today? Has anything gotten less expensive?"* (Add a personal story, if you like.)

The Pros/Cons Script

This close is especially effective in complex situations where there are a confusingly large number of considerations for the buyer to think about. All you do is make two lists. On one page under the heading *Pros,* take it on yourself to write all the positive reasons why they should buy.

Then write *Cons* on another sheet of paper and hand it to the prospects. Let them put down the negative reasons why they shouldn't buy.

Be well prepared to use this close. This means you'll have a long list of *pro* reasons memorized. You must have them in your head—you can't pull out a printed list and maintain the buyer's feeling that you're helping him reach a wise decision.

Here's how it works. Let's say that you're selling a new computer to automate an office.

When you reach the closing point of your selling sequence, say something like:

"I know this is a complex decision. Let's list the reasons for and against it so the picture will be clearer. On the pro side we have these reasons."

Get the pro reasons down on paper while they watch. Use the customer's viewpoint by writing *we* and *our* rather than you and your.

Pros

♦ Our operations can be summarized daily—vital to improve the quality of our decisions.

♦ Greater output per worker—important to hold down costs.

♦ Greater output per square foot of office space—important because our business is growing fast but we can't move to larger quarters in the foreseeable future.

♦ Local service center means our downtime will be minimized.

♦ Full support from supplier on training our personnel.

♦ Competitive prices.

Cons

♦ *On this page, jot down any reasons against the purchase that you know are important to the buyer. These will be things he's made such a big issue of that you can't overlook them. When you have those reasons noted down, stop and offer the cons sheet to him.*

♦ *The buyer may prefer that you write the cons as well as the pros. If so, do it without reluctance—otherwise you're likely to lose control and have the entire script peter out without reaching conclusion. You have to keep this concept moving or they'll start talking about something else.*

Have faith. If you know and believe in your offering, you'll be able to prepare a far longer list of pro reasons than any cons list a buyer can think of offhand.

The important thing here is truth. When you have the courage to listen to the good with the bad when dealing with the customer, the truth always wins. Remember I mentioned what you "resist— persists." A lot of times a salesperson tries to resist the worries that the buyer has all the way up to the closing sequence. I know we did a section on objections but once again the pros and cons may come up in the closing sequence. Putting them on paper and dissecting them helps. Also, have a speech prepared to tie all of this together. Try this:

"Well, it looks like the pros far exceed the cons. And some of the negatives that you brought up will be far from your thinking in three months when you see the increase in productivity."

If the system has to be special ordered be sure to use the *or* solution. *"Since this system must be special ordered, what delivery would you like? 30 or 60 days?"*

The Dollar Is It Script

The more complicated the proposition you're offering, the more important it is to quantify the reasons yea and nay. Sophisticated buyers won't compare apples to oranges. This means that to use

The Dollar Is It Script effectively with high-level prospects, you have to weigh each reason on a common scale. In most situations the only common factor that makes sense is dollars.

Let's rework the first question using the previous example from the pros list to see how this is done. Reason: Our operations can be summarized daily—vital to improve the quality of our decisions.

Your comment: *"What value should we assign to better decisions made faster, Mr. Buyer? We both know that decisions aren't likely to be any better than the information they are based on.*

"Could the better decisions that faster information will make possible add $1 million a year to your sales? If so, let's say that 10 percent of the added sales comes down to the bottom line. If you're comfortable with that figure, let's write down a dollar value of $100,000 a year to this pro reason for ordering the computer system."

As you can see, practically everything can have a dollar value put on it. Do this well before your sales interview so that you can become thoroughly familiar with every number. Then go through your entire list of pro reasons again and decide exactly what you're going to say about each one of them.

Put conservative dollar values on your pro reasons—inflated figures won't be believed or acted upon. Develop two sets of numbers for both benefits and costs: (1) Compute them on a yearly or monthly basis. (2) Compute the totals over the expected useful life of the product.

Use round numbers to help the prospects grasp your points. With buyers who are detail oriented, pull out your pocket calculator and get as far down into the fractions of pennies as they want to go.

Do a solid job of preparing this close and you'll have a tremendously powerful selling tool—one that will make you a lot of money.

The I Hope We Have It/Or I Can Get It Script

Remember the Cabbage Patch doll episode? Talk about scarcity. No one could find one of those dolls. Those that could flew in airplanes, stood in lines and beat down doors. With interest, I watched a man on T.V. tell the story of his Cabbage Patch doll. He waited in line two and a half hours in Fort Worth, Texas, because "That's what my little girl wanted for Christmas." When asked where his daughter spotted the doll, the father retorted "On T.V." Advertising is a powerful tool.

If your company does major T.V. or print advertising, realize the edge you have and use it in all your scripts. It brings up sales and causes scarcity.

Scarcity is the most important factor in antiques, gems, fine art, and collectibles of all kinds. Many companies in these fields use scarcity as their primary marketing appeal and some deliberately create it.

"Limited edition. The mold will be destroyed after only 23 copies are cast."

"Only five more building lots in this prestigious location."

"The only one of its kind in existence."

All these approaches have a common theme: "Get it now or you'll lose out—you won't have another chance." This emotion can be readily applied as a close in many other kinds of sales—if in truth the supply really is jeopardized.

Since almost every product can be obtained if the buyer is willing and able to pay enough, fear of scarcity translates readily into fear of having to pay a higher price or do without. Even on ordinary commodities (such as gasoline during the oil embargo), this can become a very real fear where the buyer can't conceive of an acceptable alternative.

How do you use the **I Hope We Have It Script** without resorting to the oldtime high pressure tactics that are so likely to make enemies? Be scrupulously honest. As long as you do that, you'll continue to build the long-term relationships with buyers that are the source of lasting sales success.

"I don't want to sound like I'm crying wolf but I'm really concerned about a strike. No one knows what will happen of course. Would you prefer having the materials for your project delivered right away or should we hold them for you in our warehouse?"

"At the rate our schedule for June is filling up, we'll have that month closed out in another 10 days, maybe sooner. July is already heavily

booked. Would you like to have a June delivery or would you prefer that I check back with you later about August?"

Any speakers reading this book will know the power of this script to tie down a speaking engagement.

Only the Chosen Ones Script

Successful insurance salespeople often use this one. They ask their prospects for a list of people who can recommend them to the insurance company. They also question whether the person they're trying to sell insurance to can qualify by passing the required physical examination.

Salespeople for houses, automobiles, boats and all kinds of major ticket items can also use this script by bringing the prospect's ability to pay into question.

Obviously this must be done tactfully or the prospect will take offense and your chances of selling that person will vanish. The safest way to work through this delicate matter is to have a form that must be filled out.

This script is then applied by studying the completed form carefully with a dubious expression on your face. After several quiet minutes, say, *"Well, I think this will fly. Let me go and check. They won't look at a tentative order of course so please approve it right here."*

When you began studying the form, your prospect was sitting there trying to make up his mind whether to take the big plunge and buy what he wants and can afford but may not absolutely have to have. Now you've switched him from worrying about the decision to worrying whether he can qualify. Very few genuine buyers will refuse to sign the order at this point.

The riskiest part of the sale is the closing sequence. And this is the sequence we most fear and love. It's like the excitement of a roller coaster. We know we are coming to the biggest dip very soon and we keep waiting for it and waiting for it with thrilled but feared anticipation. The close is the same way. Boy, I use to get excited when I would get rolling down that last hill with the customer. I knew I was now home free and we were all enjoying the ride.

The most important thing I want to leave you with in this chapter is to reiterate once again how much the *buyer hates mystery and darkness*. Let me liken it to a recent experience I had on a Delta Airline flight. Delta has always been one of my favorite airlines. They continually go the extra mile. Well, this one day, we were taxiing out of the airport towards the runway and suddenly they turned around and went back. Do you know how nervous that makes fliers? The pilot got on the microphone immediately and stated, "One of the mechanics watching the plane move out thought that the left front tire was low in air and suggested it be checked." We all thought, "Boy, they sure want to make sure we are safe before the flight, don't they?" He even said something to that effect. Compare this to another flight I took. The plane went up in the air and immediately came down and landed. No one said a word to the passengers. We looked out the window and saw a million fire trucks waiting for us. The passengers were getting crazier and crazier. Stewardesses were saying nonsensical things like, "We are going to switch you to another aircraft." Not telling us why about drove us crazy. Finally, the pilot said they thought there was something wrong with the right engine because the red light in the cockpit flashed, but then again, the wire could be faulty. Talk about a poor close. That's like the salesperson saying to the buyer, "I'm not sure if this works or not but take it home and try it and we will figure it out from there." Don't laugh. Remember that's how I was sold a portable typewriter!

People hate to be manipulated, treated like little children, talked down to or used. The close is fun and exciting as long as you keep them out of the dark. Keep picturing my Andy at the front door. The brightest smile, the most expressive eyes and happiest personality I have ever seen telling me, "Betty thought you might be dying to try this, too . . . !"

CHAPTER 9

THE LINGERING STYLE—
AFTER-SALE TECHNIQUES

Gifts, and Outrageous Ways of Giving Them ◆ *Follow Up with Ferocity* ◆ *Keep Those Cards and Letters Coming . . .* ◆ *Newsletters Sometimes Get the Job Done* ◆ *Be Consistent*

The path a natural creates to super natural status is built by one customer at a time. I look back to that first sale and remember my customer John Doyle with such fond memories. He was an executive at the time for Kodak Corporation. Not only did I sell John and his family a dream but he continued to be a source of tremendous business for me through the years. The world of Kodak was opened up because of his word of mouth. I can still remember dropping by the first Christmas they lived in their house with a special Christmas remembrance. It certainly wasn't expensive. I was so broke. I found a person who carved homemade ornaments and painted it with lots of color and inscribed the Doyles' name on the ornament. I stopped by right before Christmas and told them to hang that ornament each year and remember me. They seemed to love being remembered. The few other customers I had at the time got the same personalized gift. When you sell your product, service or company to other individuals, you are really selling them something of yourself, your personality— let's say your style. The true natural has a lingering style. It lives on long after the commission money has been spent and the final handshake has been made. We will try to give you lots of ideas that fit in with your personality to create your own personalized lingering style in this section. It's the after-sale techniques that keep you in the mind's eye of the customer.

GIFTS, AND OUTRAGEOUS WAYS OF GIVING THEM

Stopping by with gifts to customers has gone on for years. As a child, I can remember our doorbell going a mile a minute between the first and twenty-fourth of December with gifts to my dad and our family from all the distributers he did business with in those days. Bottles of wine, all types of beer and liquor, cheese baskets, candy baskets, jellies and favorite preserves, books or clocks, you name it. But the favorite stuff of all (besides the goodies) were the real personal displays of love. Like the "This Is Your Life" scrapbook that a customer put together one year for his birthday. This customer, an old friend and client of Dad, knew a lot about his background. Included were crazy pictures and thoughts that only a person who treasured Dad's business could come up with.

Some of the wonderful things you can do for your customers can include dressing up like the Easter Bunny or Santa Claus and visiting the people right at their house or inviting them to your office for a "free" picture taking session with Santa Claus. One free photo is then delivered shortly before Christmas to their door. As a salesperson, I use to appear the day the buyers were moving into their new house (this was the sixteenth transfer for the wife) with a huge carton of groceries to get the family going—breakfast cereal, milk, fruit, prepared frozen chicken, etc. Then after delivering the goodies, I told them they didn't have to use it that night because a dinner for two was set up for them at the local, restaurant. Don't make it too fancy; a lot of people are in jeans that day.

How about parties? Why not throw a big party for all your customers once a year? Maybe at Christmas. It's a great time of year and you can give them some wonderful food, drink, hospitality, and the reminder that you always appreciate their business. Can you afford trips? If you are a frequent flier on any of the airlines and don't want to use up the travel hours on yourself, why not send a valued customer and wife to an exotic place?

I knew of a lady who loved Engelbert Humperdinck. She was elderly but wealthy and a great customer of a friend of mine. The salesperson arranged with her family on her birthday to get her on an airplane at a certain time—and didn't tell her where she was going—(all the stewardesses were clued in and sang happy birthday in the first class section). When she arrived at her destination, she was escorted by limousine to the hotel where Engelbert was performing. She was ushered to the first row, not knowing who would be appearing. The opening song was her favorite—"After The Loving"—dedicated to her, of course. She was overwhelmed. How can your style not linger when you take the time to plan things like that for your customers. Now granted the larger the ticket item, the more you can afford these wayout promotions. But even if you market small products, be creative. Maybe you sell cosmetics. Maybe a regular customer of yours loves theater. Perhaps the local community group are putting on *Oklahoma*. Send two complimentary tickets to your customer. The point is take time to find out what they love and then pursue that type of a remembrance or gift for them. It isn't so much the expense of the gift but the thought behind it. I am sure my dad's "This Is Your Life" scrapbook was relatively inexpensive, but what a lasting gift.

Don't forget all the zany services provided today: belly dancers, tap dancers, singers, balloon-a-grams, breakfast in bed services, mystery train trips, etc. The list goes on and on. Our banker sent us to a place called "Magic Island" one evening. It was a special private club and restaurant that she belonged to. There were magicians, card readers, psychics, and constant entertainment going on all evening to keep you amused. We had heard about Magic Island and casually mentioned it one day while in the bank because we had seen it in the paper. Not knowing she was a member, seven months later a special delivery came to the door— tickets for two with a special pass for Magic Island any day that week we wanted to go.

FOLLOW UP WITH FEROCITY

Probably the biggest difference between the natural and the super naturals in selling is the followup. To the ordinary everyday salespeople, this contact or this sale is just another means of pay. To the super naturals, it is the start of a whole series of events after the sale. The followup for the super naturals can be as organized or unorganized as possible. The point is—just follow up. That may mean that some of you have signed up with an exclusive followup system who send greeting cards and gifts at appropriate times of the year.

For others, it may mean that you put all your old customers in a Rolodex file. Once a month you work on one letter of the alphabet. You write notes or make phone calls to that group during the next two-week period. Perhaps you use sticky notes and have to attach them on refrigerators, or time planners, desk calenders, phones, jackets or whatever it takes to remind you. But you must write it down and make it visual and it will then get done. I am not going to dish out an elaborate system of how to's to you super naturals out there because I know you have your own goofy way of doing things. The point is, no matter how crazy the system (no wonder no one understands mine but me), if it gets done that's all I care about. I will tell you though that it has to be organized some place where you have easy access to names and addresses. It should be separate from your current prospective customers. You need to write things down to remind you of the birthday or special event.

A lot of super naturals prefer offbeat greeting card occasions as opposed to the typical birthday. For insurance people, the birthday card is a natural but many salespeople feel that if they do it one year and forget the next it could be bad. I prefer the "spontaneous check" method, where every so often throughout the year, I drop a Flavia card or a special note off to an old client. Often times, it comes when the customer/friend needed a quick pick-me-up anyway. I can't tell you the importance of following the old intuition. Often when someone's name pops into your mind, they have you on their mind too.

KEEP THOSE CARDS AND LETTERS COMING . . .

The secret to my good experiences with customers, both as a salesperson and a lecturer, has truly been the testimonial letter.

The third party's written approval stating I did a good job works miracles for me. We use it in direct mail pieces to new prospects.

Think notes continually. *"I was just sitting at my desk and your bright face popped into my head. Are you still enjoying the heck out of those paper airplanes I sold you? If you need any of the extra propellers I can stop by with a bunch any time. Hope Jim and the kids are great. Pass my best on to them."*

If you run into an old customer anywhere, follow it up with a note: *"Great seeing you at the PBC cocktail party. Boy, you really must be into aerobics. You are looking fit as a fiddle. I will call you in the early part of the new year for a quick lunch."*

One thing I have found with old customers: When you initiate a call or a visit—they bring business. You remind them of your product. Listen: *"By the way, Harry is dying to talk to you about an IBM Personal."* This is why it is so crazy not to constantly visit and write after-sale customers. You no longer have to prove yourself. You just have to show up or appear on the scene! People couldn't believe the referral business I had. I think they thought I was on these people like a leach. I merely took advantage of every opportunity I could to make a quick visit, phone call or follow-up note after seeing them or running into them. I know this sounds crazy but it is easy to become a super natural. So many people do only what they have to do. And usually the buck stops after the sale. So please linger awhile.

Some great phone scripts for old customers:

"Hi, Jim, just calling to see how you are doing with the product . . . (Don't ask for a thing on this one. It is strictly a social call.)

After several weeks: *"Hi, Jim. I was just sitting here going over our inventory and we have some great special prices right now. How is your supply holding up? Also, I am on the hunt for new business. I want to spread the word about this great stuff. Can you think of three people I could contact that may be interested in* _____ . (Improving their lifestyle—changing their nutritional habits—whatever the benefits are from the product.)

"Hi Jim, I wanted to let you know that this was one of my best months in my territory. You are responsible for a lot of that. Remember so and so that you recommended to me? Well, I sold them a whole system

which put me in the top ten for the month. I know you get embarrassed every time I try to get you a special gift but what do you think your wife Laura would really love? We can both surprise her? I really want to give her something meaningful that we can say we both planned."
(For the difficult gift-buying customers.)

Keep in mind that old customers are so proud of you and want to be apprised of your success. They feel that they have a special stake in that success. Why? Because it shows that they have good taste. You are tops in your field which means they must not be so dumb, because after all, they selected you to sell them something. This is one group of people you do not have to be embarrassed about ringing your own chime with. And besides that, they show the newspaper clipping (or whatever you sent them regarding your success) around like it was a picture of their grandkid.

NEWSLETTERS SOMETIMES GET THE JOB DONE

If you are in a service business (which calls for a lot of followup and education on your part) a quarterly newsletter may be the answer. Especially if you constantly have to keep the customer updated on what is new in the field. You may want to consider that as part of the after-sale setup.

BE CONSISTENT

If you do a lot of advertising or personal promotion, remember consistency is important. Maybe a slogan or something that people remember you for is part of your promotional material. Be sure that even when you make fresh current changes in your advertising or followup, it still reflects the same old you and your beliefs said in a fresh new way. I have seen people try to change their image too many times and totally confuse and lose the customer.

The most important after-sale advice I can give you goes quite simply: Treat the customer with the same zest that you did when you knew you had the sale in the bag and were about to write it up. A lot of times people treat the early stages of selling with the same enthusiasm as the young couple who fall in love romantically and passionately. They court, marry and then wake up one day and feel like the whole thing was a bad dream. Why? Because in the beginning of a new relationship it is easy to let the sparks fly in each other's direction. But when you find yourself knee deep in housework, dirty socks and snoring one year later, everyone wants to throw in the towel.

The sale is the same way. As soon as the salesperson meets some resistance, it becomes difficult. We have to negotiate. Now the customer is not always agreeing. Maybe the emotions begin to fly. The ugly side of personalities isn't as pleasant as the early surface greeting. That's when the true bond becomes ingrained between people when they can rise above the pettiness and see the goodness of all parties.

Think of folks you have done business with for years. They aren't just people in business; they are cherished friends. Remember the local butcher who has ordered your turkey for 25 years? The dentist who put your braces on; now he's doing the same thing to your 14-year-old. The insurance man that is white at the temples who wrote you your first policy after the honeymoon was over. You wouldn't think of changing to another agent. He was there at the funeral when your mom died. He calls from time to time to "just see how you are doing." These are the *quiet super naturals* that have been there with that lingering style for decades. The whole family knows their telephone voice, or their knock at the front door. We look forward to Christmas when they appear with the favorite Wisconsin cheese packet. It takes years to build that kind of aura and presence. You can start today. Linger a while—20, 30, or 40 years in the selling industry and watch the emotional benefits it brings.

CHAPTER **10**

FIT TO SELL

How's Your Spread Sheet? ◆ *Get the Heart Rate Up* ◆ *Stretch It Out* ◆ *Mentally I Am Not as Senile* ◆ *It Relieves Depression Too* ◆ *Strengthen Your Back* ◆ *Don't Overdo* ◆ *Eat Right* ◆ *Thank You for Not Smoking* ◆ *There Is No Magic Pill or Pixie Dust*

Probably one of the most difficult tasks in the world is to stand up in front of a group and give a speech. They say that on a list of horrible fears, that's right up on top. Also included in scary stuff is giving up the security of a real job and becoming a commissioned salesperson. You wake up each morning and you are never sure what will happen. Of course, the risk is high but so are the rewards. Where else in the world can you climb to the emotional and financial peaks that selling offers. Look at some of the greats in our country: Richard DeVoss, Joe Girard, Tom Hopkins, Mary Kay, Ebbie Halliday, Ray Kroc, etc. The list goes on and on. Most of them have a rags to riches story. They started with nothing and built something!

As risky and courageous as this profession is, I could list names of people who have died early and hurt themselves physically and mentally because of the pressure of the selling field. I think of my dad, Joe Barrett; my uncle, John Barrett; and my father-in-law, Bob Craig. All these men were considered in their own way— good salespeople. But none of them made it much past sixty years old. Why? In my opinion, they weren't *fit to sell*. Being fit to sell is both a mental and physical thing. Anyone who reads this book might have picked up some good selling ideas, but the important thing is to stay alive and well to enjoy the field until a ripe old age. There are certain things in our world that we can't control.

154

Red lights that stop things include: season changes, deadlines, school starts, death, sickness and unpredictables. There are a whole bunch of green lights which we can control and that's what I want to leave you dreaming about.

HOW'S YOUR SPREAD SHEET?

Your spread sheet is a nice way of saying your back side. I know about the spread sheet because when the weight comes on that's where it goes. As a writer, I find myself glued to a chair for hours typing books or talking on the phone. As a salesperson, I would end up in the office with customers doing paperwork. Finally I would realize I was starving to death. If someone was going to the corner, I'd ask them to get me a fast food fried treat and soda pop. Of course, I would power it down the windpipe. I noticed (after living like this for several years) each afternoon I would get the "blas" bad. I would want to go in a corner and find a soft pillow to sleep on. Plus my pimple breakouts at thirty-five reminded me of when I was sixteen. I had the worst diet you could imagine. My idea of physical fitness was lifting my wrist to grab a pencil.

The next thing you know, I started making speeches. That was even more public, more risky and more insecure than selling. As a matter of fact, it's selling on a higher level. Instead of selling myself to a couple, I was now selling to an audience of one thousand. Mix travel up in this mess add the fact that I was a wife and a mom trying to do a juggling act every day of my life.

About this point, the fitness craze started. Aerobics classes started popping up all over. I also went to see Jane Fonda in *On Golden Pond*. Someone said the woman was forty and I almost died when I saw that bod. But I decided if I tried I could look pretty good myself. Anyway, I started going to Kassie Fehnske's Exercise Express and loved every minute of it. That was two years ago. Today, I am stretching, jumping and lifting like I never did at age 25. I could easily do a six-mile run in 45 minutes and feel great. It's changed my energy, my endurance and most of all my spread sheet.

GET THE HEART RATE UP

Find out what your maximum heart rate should be during an aerobic exercise, and keep it up for 15 minutes a day. This will do wonders for changing your metabolism. Plus the pure sweat from running or aerobic dance will really clear up the skin.

STRETCH IT OUT

Twenty-five percent of fitness is stretching. I could never stretch out flat on a floor two years ago. But today I can. You may say so what? Well I am a lot more limber and a lot less susceptible to injury. But most of all, I feel great. My posture has improved 1OO percent. I use to be slouched over talking on the phones to customers or feeding babies. No more. I will wager that I have stretched out a half an inch to increase my height. I can breathe better too.

MENTALLY I AM NOT AS SENILE

Just kidding of course. I am not senile yet. But as a busy sales-person, I was starting to get that way. I was forgetting phone numbers, talking to myself more (notice I said more—I still do it a little) and generally feeling foggy. The blood rushing to the head and the aerobic dancing really picked me up mentally.

IT RELIEVES DEPRESSION TOO

I am not a doctor but all I go by in this book is what is true for me. I am definitely happier and more at peace since I started my workouts. Being half Irish and half Italian in descent, I must admit that one of my weaknesses is temper. I rarely get upset, but when I do, I go off like a bomb. Going off like a bomb means that I raise the voice beyond normal tones and tend to feel sorry for myself over nothing. The workout has helped me combat that temper. It's a great way to channel anger. Many things are beyond our control in the selling field. Will a buyer be disloyal? How many complaint calls do we have to cope with today? None of the orders arrived for delivery? Human beings love to complete what they start. Frustration sets in when they are not allowed to finish a project. Salespeople have their share of frustrations daily. Use a workout to handle that negative energy.

STRENGTHEN YOUR BACK

As you know by now, I have had a few kids. Every now and then as a salesperson, when I would sit for hours, the lower back would begin to fire up on me. Doing the situps in the workout is tremendous for strengthening the back.

DON'T OVERDO

I am definitely not a physical fitness expert. So any type of activity that you are about to undertake should be cleared with your doctor. Plus you should have a good physical. All I want you to do is read this and start thinking, "Hey, I am kind of in a rut sitting on the phones and at the desk all day long. I better do something about this."

EAT RIGHT

Read some books on nutrition. Sugar is now considered a poison according to a lot of experts. Fats, oils and starches can make you feel full only temporarily. Get on a vegetable and fruit kick. Eat everything but do it in moderation. Too much of anything is bad. Get smart on this subject fast if you want increased energy throughout your selling day.

THANK YOU FOR NOT SMOKING

I also know that I have no business preaching to you about smoking but let me share a personal story. My husband, Michael, smoked two to three packs of cigarettes a day for well over 25 years. A lot of salespeople, like Mike, sit with the coffee and cigarettes and go at it all day long. Our business is nerve wracking. In between agreements, we get uptight. Many people then light up. About two years ago, Mike began to develop a very scary cough, the kind of cough that was waking him up in the middle of the night and not letting him sleep. His mother died early of emphysema and so did his dad. Well, I hate to say it but I began weeping and gnashing my teeth about his smoking. "You are going to die early and ruin this wonderful life we share. You'll miss being a grandpa." He said I was truly obnoxious but two years later he thanked me. He quit cold turkey. The first time he quit, he said he didn't smoke for two years and missed it every minute. This time he said he was well rid of the cravings. What a relief to know my chances of having him longer have gone up.

I know people have to be motivated themselves. You can't change a habit unless you want to, but it helps having someone who cares bug you a little. It also helps when someone shares the pain and admits it's tough in the beginning. Betty Ford has been a great ambassador of good news for those trying to beat the alcohol habit. It's people like Betty sharing part of their pain that make the first step to recovery possible for many others.

THERE IS NO MAGIC PILL OR PIXIE DUST

Physical fitness comes from making the effort to pick a sport or exercise you enjoy. The more you do it, the more it becomes a habit. Mental fitness is the same way. When you begin to train your mind and control the thoughts that are a part of it, you make some new mental habits.

As a kid, I was the first one in line to see *Peter Pan*. I loved the pixie dust and the idea of going to Never, Never Land for perfect happiness. But as I got older I knew that it was all just a fairy tale. There is no pixie dust or a magic pill that someone gives you. Do you realize the number of adults that are looking for that magic pill? Their minds are not fit. They have trained themselves to expect someone to give them the magic any day. Many opportunities have passed these expectant ones by. Anytime that someone did give them a break, it was usually a disappointment because it was not as great as they anticipated it would be. Losing the expectant attitude about life and your sales career is as important as doing a physical workout. So how do you do a mental workout? Live in the present moment as we discussed in chapter two. Control thoughts that come into your head that say, What can you do for me today, world? The experience of life teaches you to shed a lot of that expectancy. Believe me, I speak from experience.

In the winter of 1978, I spent Christmas alone with my children as a single parent. I was use to the traditional family life and that year I found myself divorced, grieving for my dad who had just died, and re-examining a lot of things about my life that I felt were out of balance. That year I got the message. There is no Santa Claus. No one gave me a magic pill, either. It was now up to me.

I began to understand that this world wasn't created to revolve around me. I could make mistakes just like other people. I no longer felt I had a right to be so judgmental. I also began seeing the God-given talents I had in a proud but humble way. I knew that I had to try to make the most of those talents, not only for my sake, but also for my children's sake. What I was *saying* wasn't going to cut it with them. What I was *doing* for me and them would. I also thanked God for the mistakes of that year. I began to realize that all my early successes didn't teach me half as much as my failures had. I knew I was becoming "real" and through my tears I could feel a new day coming.

That new day has arrived for me. I count myself now as one of the super naturals, totally equipped to write every page in this book from the heart. It's not theory. It's a philosophy that has been derived from everyday, on-the-job, hands-to-the-grindstone living. I look back at moments I have had with customers and I look back at moments on the stage with you. I get a feeling inside. I know other super naturals have experienced the same thing. I ask myself, "Is this really me right now saying these words so naturally and so in tune with what I am doing? Or is it my spirit dancing to a super natural song that plays in my heart? Can I keep the song going? Sure I can, because it's uniquely my song and I know I'm touching others." What about you out there behind the desk, in your territory or writing the order? Are you just doing the minimal? Are you waiting for Tinker Bell to come and sprinkle pixie dust on you and make everything okay? And let's say that Tinker Bell could come and sprinkle you with a little dust. Wouldn't it take the risk, fun, adventure and surprise out of each day? Sure sometimes we all wish we could have a little pixie dust, but do we really need it? Be counted among those who stretch and burn. Make more than just an effort. Take a natural situation and earmark it for super natural results.

Danielle Kennedy conducts lectures around the world. A complete sales training program entitled "Super Natural Selling" is available for both individual and company use on audio cassettes. When time allows, Danielle is available for customized video programs for corporations or groups.

For more information regarding speaking engagements, her books, cassette programs, time planners and other products contact:

Danielle Kennedy Productions
P.O. Box 4382
San Clemente, California 92672
(714) 498-8033